The Printer
& the Pardoner

The Printer
& the Pardoner

An Unrecorded Indulgence Printed by William Caxton

for the Hospital of St. Mary Rounceval, Charing Cross

PAUL NEEDHAM

Library of Congress · Washington · 1986

LIBRARY OF CONGRESS CATALOGING-IN-PUBLICATION DATA

Needham, Paul, 1943–
    The printer & the pardoner.

    Includes bibliographical references and index.
    Supt. of Docs. no.: LC 1.2:P93/5
    1. Caxton, William, ca. 1422–1491.   2. Hospital of
St. Mary Rounceval.   3. Broadsides—15th and 16th cen-
turies.   4. Indulgences—England—History.   5. Hospi-
tals, Medieval—England—History.   6. Printing—
England—History—15th century.   7. Rosenwald,
Lessing J. (Lessing Julius), 1891–1979—Library.
8. Library of Congress. Rare Book and Special Collections
Division.   I. Title.   II. Title: Printer and the pardoner.
Z232.C38N44   1986   686.2′092′4   85–18120
ISBN 0–8444–0508–6 (alk. paper)

♾ The paper used in this publication meets the requirements
for permanence established by the American National Standard for
Information Sciences "Permanence of Paper for Printed Library Materials"
(ANSI Z39.48–1984).

Contents

Illustrations

The drawings for figures 2, 4, 5, and 6 are by Margaret R. Brown.

Preface

IN THE SPRING of 1980, Paul Needham, curator of printed books and bindings at the Pierpont Morgan Library, made a discovery of major consequence at the Library of Congress. While examining the paper in one of the finest volumes in the Lessing J. Rosenwald Collection, a volume containing four separate editions printed by William Caxton, England's first printer, he found an unknown fifth Caxton item buried in the volume as sewing strips. Further investigation identified the text as a broadside indulgence printed by Caxton for the hospital of St. Mary Rounceval. The Center for the Book commissioned Mr. Needham to prepare this book about the Rounceval indulgence and its significance.

Mr. Needham made his discovery just as the Library of Congress was focusing attention on the Rosenwald Collection and on its potential value to researchers. The exceptional collection of twenty-six hundred books that Lessing J. Rosenwald donated to the Library of Congress beginning in 1943 is distinguished for its value to scholarship, for the beauty of the volumes, and for the many and varied illustrations found within them. In May 1980 the Library honored Mr. Rosenwald, who had died the previous year, with an interdisciplinary symposium that demonstrated the scholarly potential of this collection. The papers commissioned from art historians, cartographers, and bibliographers were published in *The Early Illustrated Book: Essays in Honor of Lessing J. Rosenwald*, edited by Sandra Hindman, in 1982. The Rounceval indulgence so clearly described and analyzed by Paul Needham exemplifies yet another kind of discovery waiting to be made in this rich resource.

Initiated by the Center for the Book, *The Printer & the Pardoner* represents a cooperative effort among several Library of Congress departments. The Rare Book and Special Collections Division, home of the Rosenwald Collection, lent its assistance at every stage of the project. The Preservation Office skillfully removed the strips from the Caxton volume to facilitate Mr. Needham's research, and the Publishing Office gave his manuscript the careful attention it deserved. Support for the publication was provided by the Clapp Publication Fund, established in honor of Verner W. Clapp, Chief Assistant Librarian of Congress, upon his retirement from the Library in 1956 after a long and distinguished career. The fund was recently enhanced by a publication fund given to the Library by Lessing J. Rosenwald, so its use here is particularly fitting. The Center for the Book is especially grateful to William Matheson, chief of the Rare Book and Special Collections Division, for suggesting the project and of course to Paul Needham for agreeing to undertake it.

Encouraging the study of the history of books is a principal aim of the Center for the Book. Created by Act of Congress in 1977 to stimulate public interest in books, reading, and the printed word, the center is an informal, voluntary organization funded primarily by private contributions. It brings together members of the book, educational, and business communities for projects and events that enhance books and reading. Drawing on the collections of the Library of Congress, its projects consider books in their varied roles—as physical objects, as exemplars of the graphic and typographic arts, as transmitters of ideas, and as influences on society. It is a pleasure to present Paul Needham's important contribution to Caxton studies and book history to a wider audience.

John Y. Cole
Executive Director
The Center for the Book

The Printer
& the Pardoner

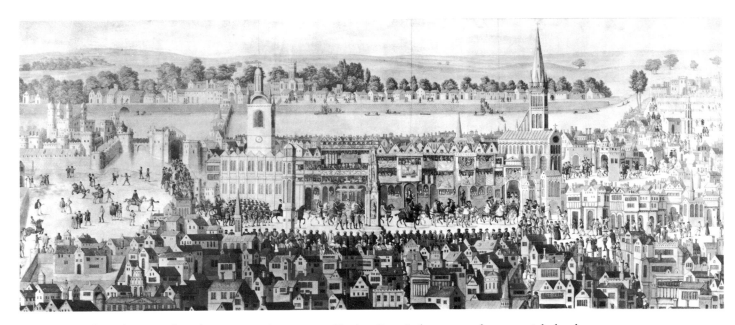

FIG. 1   View from the City of London to Westminster, 1547. Charing Cross is shown near the upper right border.

William Caxton, England's First Printer

MONARCHS AND MAGNATES APART, William Caxton (ca. 1420–1491) is today probably the best-known and most widely honored Englishman of his century. All of Caxton's fame depends on the activities of the last two decades of his life. Before then, he was a cloth merchant, living abroad in the Low Countries, where he amassed considerable wealth and a considerable influence in the English alien merchant community. Caxton's position as governor of this community in Bruges involved him, at times, in diplomatic and quasi-diplomatic services to the English crown. These worthy actions enrolled his name in various documents still extant—in a small way, Caxton's mercantile and diplomatic careers have left their traces in history—but there was nothing in any of this to make later centuries specially remember him.

Then, when he was almost fifty years old, Caxton took up, in midst of his various responsibilities, a literary pastime. He began a translation into English of a currently fashionable Franco-Burgundian text, Raoul Le Fèvre's *Recueil des histoires de Troye*, which recast the ancient legends of the Trojan war into late medieval chivalric conventions. Caxton intended to dedicate his English rendering to Margaret of York, sister of the English king, Edward IV, and bride of the duke of Burgundy, Charles the Bold. Le Fèvre's *Recueil* had only a few years earlier been dedicated to Charles's father, the late duke Philip the Good, so it is easy to understand Caxton's reasoned hope that his literary token would win the duchess's approval.

Toward the end of 1470, before Caxton had finished his translation, some political reversal seems to have lost him his influential position in Bruges. He moved to Cologne, where he lived in exile or retirement for the next year and a half. Shortly after arriving there, Caxton completed his version of Le Fèvre's *Recueil* (September 1471). Cologne, a thriving, populous commercial city and archiepiscopal see on the lower Rhine, was developing at this time into one of the most important centers of the new German invention, printing. Caxton's decision to involve himself in this rapidly expanding area of the book trade oriented his life in a new direction. It must soon have occurred to him (if indeed this did not supply the primary motivation) that his newly completed translation of the Troy story would be an impressive thing in print. As a perfected technology, Gutenberg's invention was less than two decades old, and it had just in the previous five or six years begun to spread widely from its birthplace in Mainz. No Englishman had as yet learned the art of printing, nor had German craftsmen skilled in printing as yet made their way to the British isles.

During his sojourn in Cologne, Caxton engaged a printing shop to work on commission for him, producing anonymously a large and expensive book, the encyclopedia of Bartholomaeus Anglicus, *De proprietatibus rerum*. After this ambitious project was completed, Caxton returned in early 1473 to Bruges, where he set up that town's first press, using a type specially designed for his requirements. The first book Caxton completed in Bruges was his translation for Margaret of York, the *Recuyell of the Histories of Troy*; this was the first book printed in English. It was soon followed, in early 1474, by another of Caxton's own translations, the *Game of Chess* of Jacobus de Cessolis. In the next year or two Caxton printed four more books in Bruges, all texts in French, the cultivated language of the region. They are among the earliest examples of printing in French.

In 1476, Caxton returned to England after decades abroad, and reestablished his printing shop, the first to be located on English soil, at Westminster Abbey. There he spent the remainder of his life. In these fifteen years he produced about one hundred still-surviving pieces of printing, ranging in size and scale from small broadsides of a few lines each to the giant large-folio collection of saints' lives, the *Golden Legend*. Among his most important publications were the first editions of Chaucer's *Canterbury Tales*, and of Sir Thomas Malory's *Morte d'Arthur*. Caxton is a unique figure among the early printers because of the great quantity of material he personally prepared for publication, including his own translations from French, Dutch, and Latin. These translations, and Caxton's editions of such important native authors as Chaucer, Lydgate, Gower, and Malory, show that the chief (though not the sole) emphasis of his enterprise was placed on providing vernacular literary texts for a lay readership, rather than learned reference texts in Latin or Law French for the professional use of clerks and legists. As a group, Caxton's editions are also unique among early printed books in being so frequently provided with long, chatty prologues and epilogues, often written with conscious humor, in which Caxton explained the occasions and circumstances of his publications. These were written with an eye to good publicity in their time, and they are still excellent reading today. No other printer in the fifteenth century spoke so directly and ingratiatingly to his audience as did Caxton, and as a result he still speaks to us today in a way that no other early printer does.

Of the hundred and more books and broadsides produced by Caxton, most were recorded already in the eighteenth century by the antiquary historians of early English printing Joseph Ames and William Herbert. By the end of the nineteenth century, in consequence particularly of the scholarship of William Blades and Henry Bradshaw, the list of Caxton's output was essentially complete. But discoveries of unrecorded work by Caxton have continued to be made, although at a much slower rate, in this century .What follows is the story of one such discovery, minor but satisfying, and not entirely negligible in the additional light it sheds on several aspects of Caxton's trade.

The Rosenwald Sammelband and Other Caxton Tract Volumes

ONE OF THE FINEST surviving volumes of Caxton's printing first came to light in London, in a Sotheby auction of 20–21 May 1909, lot 493. The volume contained, in an early binding, four separate folio editions from William Caxton's press. These were:

1. *The Mirror of the World*, tr. Caxton. [ca. September 1481]. 100 leaves. Duff 401, Goff M-883.
2. *Dicts and Sayings of the Philosophers*, tr. Anthony, Earl Rivers. Second edition. [ca. June 1480]. 78 leaves. Duff 124, Goff D-273.
3. Cicero, *Of Old Age*; Cicero, *Of Friendship*; and Bonacursius de Montemagno, *Of Nobility*. 12 August 1481. 120 leaves. Duff 103, Goff C-627.
4. *Cordiale of the Four Last Things*, tr. Anthony, Earl Rivers. 24 March 1479. 78 leaves. Duff 109, Goff C-907.

There is no entirely satisfactory term in English for volumes of this character, containing a number of separable books, whether printed or manuscript, within a single pair of covers. They have at various times and in various contexts been referred to as tract, pamphlet, or composite volumes. Such phrases suggest, to my ears, the seventeenth and eighteenth centuries, when sermons or poems, commonly of pamphlet length, were commonly so bound. They have a slightly anachronistic ring when applied to fifteenth- and early sixteenth-century volumes, which often contained—witness the volume just described—quite substantial editions, such as in later times would have been sold and bound as separate units. The German word for such volumes is *Sammelband*, and despite its rather outlandish sound, it has this advantage, that it does not, like *tract volume*, imply that only slight works would be bound together in this way.

Sammelbände were once common for a simple reason: until the nineteenth century, generally speaking, there was no such thing as a ready-bound edition, corresponding to the clothbound books with which we (in English-speaking countries) are familiar today. From the invention of printing through the eighteenth century, copies of books were almost invariably supplied to booksellers either in sheets or gathered into flimsy wrappers as a temporary makeshift. Binding took place in the individual bookshops, usually at the time of sale, and the binding would be an extra expense for the customer, additional to the cost of the sheets themselves. A reader who bought three or four or more books at the same time and in the same format might naturally choose to have them bound up together, rather than pay the labor and materials for three or four separate bindings.

Many fifteenth-century books in general, and many examples of Caxton's printing in particular, were once in Sammelbände but are so no longer. In the eighteenth and nineteenth centuries, early printed books increasingly attracted the attention of antiquarian bibliophiles.

In England, the productions of the nation's first and greatest printer, William Caxton, naturally enjoyed particular favor. Such favor, which must have prevented the destruction by negligence of many of Caxton's books, was not, however, an unalloyed good. Collectors of Caxton wanted their volumes to look neat and trim and to stand in bindings reflecting their own, albeit temporary, possession. Almost all copies, therefore, as they came into the hands of antiquarian booksellers and clients, were cut out of old covers and put into new ones. More often than not, the leaves were washed, bleached, and pressed, to remove stains and annotations (or, if the copies were imperfect, to render less conspicuous the contrast between authentic leaves and inserted facsimiles) and to make them lie flat; edges were trimmed and gilded; modern covers of various inappropriate designs were put on, usually with exceedingly tight backs, preventing the books from opening properly. The result was inevitably something smaller, thinner, meaner, and less honest than what had been before.

The species of taste that ordained such ministrations was not greatly concerned that certain copies of Caxton's editions might once have been bound together or bound with other printed books or manuscripts. A curiosity about such potential clues to the original marketing, or to the original purchasers, of Caxton's books was alien to the mentality of the eighteenth- and nineteenth-century connoisseur. Thus, when T. F. Dibdin, the chief apostle of this collecting movement, and deep-dyed in its precepts, discovered at York Minster a quarto volume containing two unique Caxton verse editions bound up with several contemporary Parisian editions, he at once arranged to have the volume sent to the fashionable London binder Charles Lewis, to be "dissect[ed] and cover[ed] with appropriate bindings." The instinct here, to regard it in its most favorable aspect, was to pay homage to the rarity of the books by making of each a discrete and conspicuous icon.

Less honorable motives for breaking up volumes animated, and continue to animate, bookdealers. There is a strong, persistent, and not wholly unjustified—yet at least partly self-fulfilling—belief in the trade that two valuable books bound together cannot be sold for as much as the two separately. The remedy is the knife. A dealer who resists the temptation to break up a composite volume is usually conscious of a special sense of virtue, but one cannot expect dealers always to practice conspicuous virtue at the expense of their purses. The more fundamental blame surely lies with the buyers of books: if collectors were more reluctant to acquire butchered books, many fewer would be butchered.

Furthermore, it would be quite wrong to place entire responsibility for such mishandling of books on dealers and private collectors, much less on the ignorance of a bygone age. Libraries, without the same excuses and with a much greater and more direct responsibility for the care of their holdings, have likewise often been guilty of disbinding volumes that should have been preserved as entities. Perhaps the greatest of all Caxton-related volumes was one acquired in the late seventeenth or early eighteenth century by John Moore, bishop of Ely. In 1715, by the benefaction of George I, the volume was presented with the rest of

Moore's library to Cambridge University. This volume contained eight verse quarto tracts printed by Caxton in 1477, including texts of Chaucer and Lydgate, all but one of which are (with the exception of a few fragments) unique. An entire chapter of Caxton's printing history was preserved within this pair of covers. In the nineteenth century, for reasons no longer easily ascertainable, the volume was broken up, and each title bound separately. This is not precisely comparable with book-breaking by a dealer, for these copies will always remain at Cambridge, and the history of their former association and single provenance will not be lost. But still, their integrity—and whatever evidence resided in their earlier binding—has been lost.

This is just one of many examples where disbinding has destroyed the integrity of Caxton tract volumes. In every instance, whether or not a financial motive is present, the underlying fault is a failure of historical imagination. Bishop Moore's library, when it came to Cambridge, contained another tract volume, comprising five Caxton folios, which likewise was eventually disbound. The original collector of this volume had been one R. Johnson, who wrote in each book the price he paid for it in 1510, ranging from fourpence to two shillings eightpence. Here again, one cannot help wondering, regretfully, what sort of binding this volume might have had in Bishop Moore's time, what annotations its endleaves might have borne, and so on.

The British Library's copy of Caxton's rare *Book of Good Manners* (11 May 1487) was, when acquired at the turn of the century, in a contemporary Cambridge binding, sandwiched between two other Caxton texts: the *Royal Book* (ca. 1485–86) and the *Doctrinal of Sapience* (late 1489). To help defray the expense of the acquisition, the British Museum (as it then was) had these two accompanying editions, both imperfect, cut out of the binding and returned to the bookseller as part payment. This copy of the *Doctrinal of Sapience* is today at the University of Illinois; the present location of the *Royal Book* is unknown. Curiously, Bishop Moore owned a closely similar Caxton volume, containing these same three editions plus a copy of Caxton's third edition of *Dicts of the Philosophers* (late 1489). This volume, too, was broken up after it came to Cambridge. Other copies of the *Book of Good Manners* and of the *Royal Book* are, or once were, bound with either the *Doctrinal of Sapience* or with the third edition of *Dicts*, and we very probably, in these now-dispersed survivals, possess a tenuous clue to how the texts were originally marketed. A substantial number of copies of the *Royal Book* and of *Book of Good Manners* seem to have been sold two to four years after they were printed, in 1489 and after. These late sales are very probably related in some way to a hiatus in Caxton's shop between mid-1487 and mid-1489, when he apparently, for reasons unknown, stopped printing and perhaps also stopped selling books.

Consider now another characteristic example of destruction of a Caxton Sammelband. In 1898, a beautiful folio volume came on the market containing six Caxton editions, all dating between 1482 and 1484. This volume had belonged in the eighteenth century to the antiquary Maurice Johnson of Spalding, Lincs. At the time the volume was marketed in 1898, two of its texts were removed and sold to the British Museum, and the other four went to the Christie-Miller collection at Britwell Court. These latter stayed at Britwell Court for only two decades, then returned to the market again. Two are now in the Pierpont Morgan Library, and two in the Yale Center for British Art. All six texts, which almost certainly were selected together by one of Caxton's customers in the mid-1480s, are now in separate bindings.

This by no means completes the tally of destruction. Mishandling of Sammelbände has continued very nearly as strong in recent times as it did in the bad old days of Dibdin. In the early 1950s a unique, hitherto unrecorded Caxton folio, Laurentius Traversanus's *Epitome margaritae eloquentiae* [1480], was discovered at Ripon Cathedral, in a volume containing also three continental incunables and various manuscript texts. The book, being badly water-damaged, was sent to the conservation laboratory of the British Museum for treatment. It was there disbound and was never reassembled. The non-Caxton contents were separated from the *Epitome*, and are now in other hands than those of the eventual owner of the Caxton text (Leeds University). The *Epitome* itself was rebound in such a way that its original collation, never accurately recorded, can no longer be satisfactorily reconstructed. However poor the condition of the book may have been when first discovered, its subsequent treatment, by the most respectable authorities, has resulted in the irretrievable loss of much valuable information. Many interesting questions about the history of the volume as a whole can no longer be asked.

This melancholy rehearsal of bibliographical malfeasance in re Caxton supplies a gloomy backdrop against which the volume sold by Sotheby's in 1909 stands out the more brightly. That book, the property of an anonymous "Gentleman living in an old Manor House in the North," had so far as we know never been in the antiquarian trade before. It rested peacefully in a secluded corner of Britain during the generations when its fellows were, one after another, being broken up, dismembered, facsimile'd, washed, bleached, ironed, trimmed, gilded, and generally titivated in the binderies of Roger Payne, Charles Lewis, Francis Bedford, and others. Messrs. Sotheby realized that it was (by now) a unique stroke of fortune to find four Caxton editions in a single volume, and they billed it, properly, as something extraordinary, the more so as they mistakenly believed that the binding was contemporary with the contents, rather than dating, as it actually does, to some fifty or sixty years later.

The volume was knocked down to a certain E. Stanley for the very high price of £2600. Sometime later it was bought by a New York collector, James W. Ellsworth, among whose numerous other treasures was a copy of the Gutenberg Bible in a contemporary Erfurt binding. In 1923, late in life, Ellsworth sold his library en bloc to A. S. W. Rosenbach, the leading American rare book dealer of his generation. Many of Ellsworth's incunables passed from Rosenbach into the collection of Henry E. Huntington, but the Caxton Sammelband was acquired by Charles W. Clark, brother of William Andrews Clark and like him an important collector. After C. W. Clark's death in 1933, Rosenbach served as agent for Mrs. Clark in gradually disposing of her husband's library. As it happened, the Caxton volume, the high spot of the collection, remained in Rosenbach's shop for a good many years. Finally in 1947 Lessing J. Rosenwald, long one of Rosenbach's best customers, bought it for $37,500. Rosenwald had already by that date set in motion the steps by which his extraordinary collection of books and manuscripts was to be given to the Library of Congress, and his drawings and prints to the National Gallery. I will not speak here at any length about the quality and significance of Lessing Rosenwald's library, but it should be said that at the national level, it is the most important benefaction of books that our country has ever received, or is ever likely to. In his lifetime, Mr. Rosenwald continued to keep his library by him at Alverthorpe, in the suburbs of Philadelphia, and many scholars consulted it there. After Mr. Rosenwald's death in June 1979, at the age of eighty-seven, his books were transported, as had long been planned, to the Library of Congress. Among these was the Caxton Sammelband, long one of Mr. Rosenwald's favorites.

An Unrecorded Caxton Indulgence Preserved as Binder's Waste

I FIRST SAW the Rosenwald Sammelband in the spring of 1980, a few weeks after it had arrived at the Library of Congress. My plan at that time was to make a fairly rapid survey of the fifteenth-century English printing in the Library of Congress, now greatly enriched not only by this one extraordinary volume but also by some dozen more Caxton editions from Mr. Rosenwald's library as well as a small group of English incunables from presses other than Caxton's. The primary aim of the survey was to take record of the paper stocks in the books. This was part of a long-term and still-continuing investigation I have undertaken into the dates and chronology of fifteenth-century English printing, beginning with Caxton, but including also the other early English presses: the one or two shops at Oxford; the anonymous printer at St. Albans; John Lettou and William de Machlinia in London; and the printers of the 1490s—Wynkyn de Worde, Richard Pynson, Julian Notary.

It should be explained that the majority of English incunables, and the great majority of Caxton's books, are undated. Most of these can be assigned dates to varying degrees of precision by several means. One of the most revealing items of evidence for dating early printed books is the paper they were printed on. Most fifteenth-century paper contains watermarks, that is, images formed by shaped wires sewn to the paper molds, which become

FIG. 2 Twin paper molds and their common deckle.

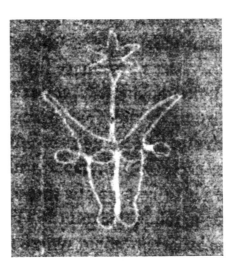

FIG. 3 Twin watermarks of a paper stock manufactured about 1480, probably in a mill near Genoa. Caxton used a substantial supply of this stock in the second half of 1481, in the printing of two books: Cicero, *Of Old Age* (Cx 45) and *Mirror of the World* (Cx 46).

visible when the paper is examined against the light. Characteristic marks of the French and northern Italian mills that supplied the English printing shops include bull's heads, hands, unicorns, and many other symbols. Each paper stock Caxton used can be defined by its watermarks. These same stocks might be used by Caxton both in his dated and undated books, and often enough they can be found in dated books from other presses, whether in England or on the Continent, for paper was marketed widely. When this complex of paper evidence is combined with a variety of other chronological clues—typographical evidence, textual evidence, progressive states of damage to printer's marks and other woodcuts, and so on—a quite reliable dated sequence for Caxton's printing can be constructed.

The four Caxton editions making up the Rosenwald Sammelband are not, as it happens, ones where paper evidence comes into play with particularly striking effect. Two of the four—the Cicero and the *Cordiale*— are precisely dated. Their colophons reveal not only the year they were printed but also the month and day on which they were completed. For one of these editions, the *Cordiale*, we also, quite remarkably, know the day on which printing was begun. Caxton's colophon tells us that Earl Rivers delivered his copy of the text on 2 February 1479, that printing began the next day, and that the work was completed just seven weeks later, on 24 March 1479. As for the edition containing translations of Cicero and Bonacursius, it too is precisely dated, but with a slight complication. This book is divided into two separable parts, and only the first part contains a specified completion date, 12 August 1481. It can be shown, however, that part 2 was printed directly after part 1, and so its completion date must also fall in 1481, probably around September.

The natural history compendium *Mirror of the World* is dated not as a printed book but as a text. Caxton records that he finished his translation of it on 8 March 1481, so the printed edition must be later than that date. Paper evidence helps in determining how much later, for it reveals that production of *Mirror* came after, not (as had previously been assumed) before, the Cicero. Since part 1 of the Cicero was finished 12 August 1481, and part 2 followed directly after, a likely production time for *Mirror of the World* is the autumn of 1481.

The most problematical of the editions in the Rosenwald Sammelband is the *Dicts and Sayings of the Philosophers*, a collection of mostly apocryphal stories about the sages of antiquity, Pythagoras, Socrates, and many another. Like the *Cordiale*, the *Dicts* was translated from the French by Earl Rivers, brother-in-law of the reigning king, Edward IV. The colophon of this edition states that it was completed on 18 November 1477. But here there is a problem. There exist in fact two editions—that is, two typographically distinct printings—of the *Dicts*, which correspond to each other page for page, both of which contain this same colophon date. It is not immediately obvious which of the two editions came first. In one of these editions, all copies save one record the date simply, on folio 74r, as 1477. The exception is a copy now in the Rylands Library, University of Manchester, which has a second colophon of 8 lines added to the last printed page (folio 76v), specifying the date as 18 November

1477. In the other of these "twin" editions of *Dicts*, all copies (including the one in the Rosenwald volume) contain the second, more specific colophon. It has long been recognized that this latter edition was copied from the former edition (more precisely, from one of the special copies of the former edition which included the additional colophon), and hence its stated date of 18 November 1477 must be incorrect.

The clearest evidence for this sequence of the two editions comes from their types. The first edition was set with Caxton's type 2, a font he used first in Bruges and then in Westminster for almost all his printing of 1476 and 1477. The second, copied edition of *Dicts* was set from a variant recasting of type 2, which is conventionally designated as 2*. This recasting was made in 1478, so the second edition of *Dicts* can be no earlier than 1478. It is at this point—for the typographical evidence can go no farther—that paper evidence proves useful in suggesting a quite precise date for the second edition of *Dicts*. The eight paper stocks found in this edition are intimately linked with those used in Caxton's edition of the *Chronicles of England*, whose colophon records its completion on 10 June 1480. It is likely that the second edition of *Dicts* was completed shortly before the *Chronicles*, and hence belongs to the spring of 1480.

I had already examined various other copies of all four of the editions in the Rosenwald Sammelband before arriving in Washington, and so was not particularly expecting surprises to emerge from it. But it is always good, and often imperative, when studying paper stocks in any detail, to look at more than one copy of a particular book. Indeed, some details of paper use may not fully reveal themselves until a dozen or more copies of a book have been examined. It is only by the compilation of such multiple records that the changes from one stock to another in the course of production can be accurately pinpointed, and this information in turn may reveal much about other aspects of the book's production.

Before I had gotten fairly started in examining and recording the sequence of paper stocks in the four books making up the Rosenwald Sammelband, a rather trivial error in the sewing of its binding caught my eye. For a clearer understanding of this error, it will be well to consider for a moment the physical structure of the Rosenwald volume. All four books in the volume are folios. This means that each of their leaves is one-half of a sheet of paper, each full sheet, measuring approximately twelve by eighteen inches, having been folded once to produce two leaves of about twelve-inch height and nine-inch width. These sheets were gathered into quires, most commonly of four sheets each (see diagram). Thus, the quire would consist of eight leaves, or sixteen pages. Pages 1 and 16 would lie on the outside of the first sheet, pages 2 and 15 on its inside, pages 3 and 14 on the outside of the second sheet, and so on.

A book was bound by stabbing a length of thread through the fold of the first quire (thus preventing its sheets from coming apart), and then looping the thread, where it emerged at the back of the quire fold, around leather thongs. Next the thread was carried up and stitched

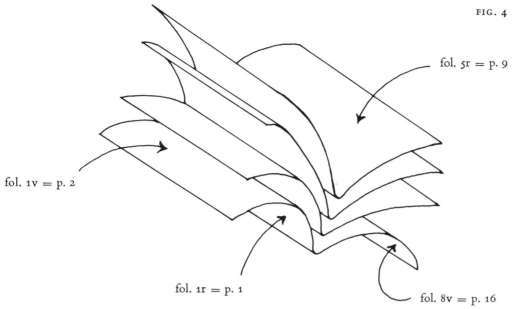

FIG. 4   A folio quire of four sheets.

fol. 5r = p. 9

fol. 1v = p. 2

fol. 1r = p. 1

fol. 8v = p. 16

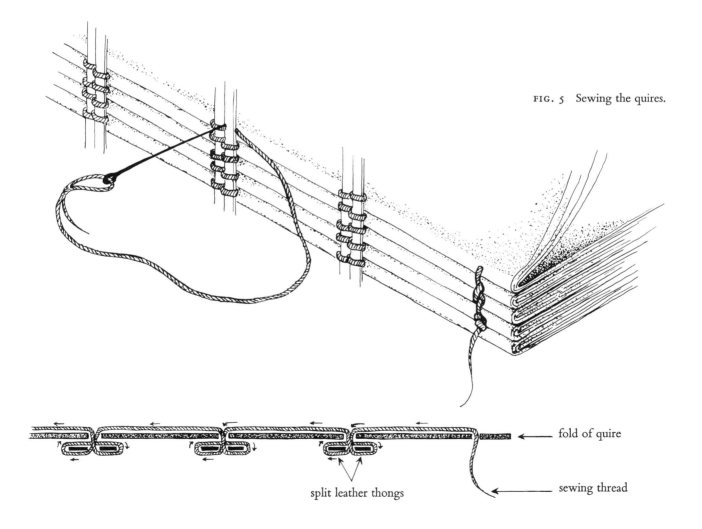

FIG. 5   Sewing the quires.

fold of quire

split leather thongs

sewing thread

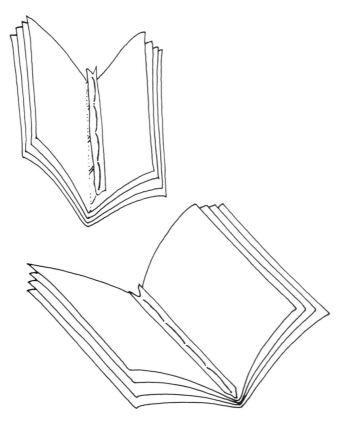

FIG. 6 Quire guards.

through the fold of the second quire, and so on. At the end of the sewing process, each quire was held together by the stitching through its fold, and all the quires were linked to one another by their common attachment to the leather thongs, which ran vertically to the quire folds (see diagram). The ends of these thongs were laced into wooden boards, and the boards were covered with leather, to form a finished bookbinding. The result was incomparably stronger than the ordinary commercial binding of today.

The first quire of the first text in the Rosenwald volume, *Mirror of the World*, contains eight leaves, the first of which is a blank (trimmed away in the Rosenwald copy). Therefore, the quire fold lies between the fourth and fifth leaves, if we include the missing blank in our count. In fifteenth- and sixteenth-century bindings, strips of vellum (or sometimes of paper) are frequently found in the quire folds (see diagram). These strips served as reinforcements or guards, preventing the threads from tearing into the fold during sewing or later when the volume was opened and flexed.

In the first quire of the Rosenwald volume, I noticed just such a strip, but it was in the wrong place. Instead of lying properly in the quire fold, it was placed between the fifth and sixth leaves, where it had no function. While pausing momentarily to ponder this—the volume, I thought (as later proved to be true), must have been disbound and reassembled fairly recently, by a modern binder who had misplaced this guard—I noticed that there was printing on the strip, on the side face down against the leaves. With a little manipulation, the first line of print, running along the length of the strip, could be exposed. It read: "Edwardus ponyngis Cappellanus domini regis, Magister siue custos, hospitalis beate et gloriose virginis Marie," that is, "Edward Poynings, chaplain of the lord king, master or custodian of the hospital of the blessed and glorious virgin Mary." The *E* of Edward was printed not with metal type but with a larger woodcut capital, suggesting that this was the opening of the text.

In the second quire there was another such strip, this time correctly sewn into the fold. It also bore printing, the first line of which could be partially read as "de Rouncideuall iuxta charingcrosse extra muros Londonii situate, Iohannes Kendale . . . ," the remainder of the line being lost in the sewing. This can be translated as "of Rounceval, situated by Charing Cross outside the walls of London, John Kendale . . . ." In fact, this line directly follows the line of the first strip, so that we have a text beginning, in English translation, "Edward Poynings, chaplain of the lord king, master or custodian of the hospital of the blessed and glorious virgin Mary of Rounceval, situated by Charing Cross outside the walls of London, John Kendale . . . ."

Similar printed vellum strips turned up in the folds of other quires: there were twelve printed strips in all, plus one strip of blank vellum, in the forty-nine quires of the entire volume. In most of the quires now lacking vellum guards, staining in the central folds showed that strips had once been present but later were lost. A number of the folds also showed, from traces of offset ink, that the missing strips had printing on them. Besides the twelve surviving printed strips, printed vellum must once have lined at least twelve other quires.

Further examination of the printing on the strips, insofar as it was visible in situ, led to the following preliminary conclusions: (1) The strips were the cut-up remains of a single piece of printing, a broadside indulgence issued by the hospital of Our Lady of Rounceval, situated near Charing Cross. (2) The indulgence was printed with one of Caxton's types, his type 4. This type was used between 1480 and early 1484. Toward the end of 1482, Caxton made a recasting of the type, with several variant letters, which is designated type 4* (on analogy with types 2 and 2*, as explained above), and type 4* was used between late 1482 and 1487. (3) But the state of the type in the indulgence was that of the original font, so on purely typographical grounds, the indulgence would be dated [ca. 1480–84]. It did not take long, moreover, to confirm that there was no other record of this printed indulgence. A previously unknown piece of printing from Caxton's shop had come to light in the Rare Book Room of the Library of Congress.

When it became known that the Rosenwald volume contained, so to speak, not four but five Caxton editions, one of which was hitherto unrecorded, the Library of Congress gave every assistance toward a more extended study of the fragments. In particular, it was agreed that the sewing of the binding should be removed one more time, permitting the strips to be taken out and more completely read. Since the present sewing of the volume was modern, and in fact as recent as the 1960s (when Mr. Rosenwald sent the volume to a Chicago bindery for repairs), this could be done without damaging or destroying any of the volume's original materials.

Once the strips were loose, it was a relatively simple matter to arrange them in order and reconstruct the greater part of the indulgence's text. It became clear that at least four copies of the indulgence had been cut up when the quire guards were originally made, for the first line of text, beginning "Edwardus ponyngis," appears wholly or partially on four of the strips. Indulgences were intended to be sold, and blank spaces were left in their texts to be filled in at the time of sale with the name of the purchaser and the date. The blank spaces in these strips were not filled in, indicating that Lessing J. Rosenwald's volume contained unsold copies. They probably (as we shall soon see) had not strayed far from Caxton's printing shop at the time they were cut up by the binder.

The first sixteen lines of the indulgence survive completely. Of line 17, only the final four words are present. There is then a gap of at least one line, but more probably of three or four lines—the amount of text that would have appeared on a single strip. Then four more lines survive completely, but the final line or two is missing. The entire indulgence, therefore, probably consisted of some twenty-six or twenty-seven lines, twenty of which survive completely and one partially in the Rosenwald volume. Before examining this particular indulgence in detail, something more general should be said about the printing of indulgences in the fifteenth century.

Early Indulgence Printing and Its Survival

VERY SOON AFTER Johann Gutenberg perfected his invention of printing with individual and reusable types, it must have become obvious that the process was beautifully adapted to producing not just books but any texts—secular and religious official documents, public announcements, advertisements, and so forth—that it was useful or necessary to have in multiple copies. Book-printing and job-printing were born together.

The first printed book, the forty-two-line or Gutenberg Bible, is undated, but we know it was well under production in the autumn of 1454 and was probably completed soon afterward. Shortly after it was finished, the business association between Gutenberg and Johann Fust broke up. In the next decade, the two men seem to have maintained separate printing

shops in Mainz, Fust in association with his son-in-law Peter Schoeffer. Before the end of 1454, both Mainz shops had issued their first (or first surviving) pieces of jobbing work in the form of indulgences whose purpose was to raise money, under papal auspices, to aid in defending the island of Cyprus from the Turkish advance. It will be recalled that just a year before this, Constantinople had fallen to the Turks.

By Catholic doctrine, an indulgence is a remission of the penalties that must be paid for one's sins, whether in this life or in purgatory. Throughout the Middle Ages, popes exercised their traditional right to grant indulgences, whose efficacy presupposed in the sinner a sincere repentance. By the late Middle Ages, indulgences of various types had become common articles of commerce, whose distribution and sale were highly organized and whose revenues were important to several branches of the church. The Cyprus indulgences, for instance, brought various sums, ranging up to eight florins for an indulgence issued to an entire convent, and the two Mainz shops might easily have printed several thousand indulgence forms for distribution through the diocese.

It must have become evident very quickly that if large sales of a particular indulgence were anticipated, the work of the pen could not effectively compete with the work of the press. Setting an indulgence text in type would have taken only an hour or two, and by the end of the day more copies would be ready for the pardoners' sacks than a scrivener could prepare in several weeks of steady writing.

Although no precise count has been made, probably about six hundred printed editions of indulgence instruments from the fifteenth century survive, more than any other single class of early job-printing. Unrecorded indulgences continue to be discovered, slowly but steadily, through just such channels as Mr. Rosenwald's volume. The number that originally existed is certainly very much greater: for every printed indulgence edition that survives, three or four or more other editions might easily have disappeared without trace.

The fate of any manuscript or printed material, before it becomes the object of specific antiquarian collecting interest, is dependent on a long series of accidents, which tend toward either preservation or destruction. A fifteenth-century book intended for sale to more or less permanent libraries—such as the writings of a church father, which would have been purchased by many monasteries and other collegiate institutions—is much more likely to have survived into the twentieth century than one intended for sale to the laity, such as a vernacular romance. As example, consider the first edition of the collected works of St. Ambrose. It was published in Basel, 1492, and survives today in more than 150 copies. This is the only recorded fifteenth-century edition of Ambrose's writings, and in light of its very high survival rate, one may feel confident in asserting that there were no other early editions of the same text, aimed at the same market, which have disappeared from historical record.

By contrast, six fifteenth-century editions are currently known of the popular French chivalric romance *Paris et Vienne*. They have a very different pattern of survival from that of the 1492 Ambrose. One edition of *Paris et Vienne* is recorded in two copies, the remainder are known by a single copy each. Given such a pattern, it could very well be that other editions of the text were printed in the fifteenth century, but have failed to survive. Indeed, if one wanted to believe that *only* these six known editions of *Paris et Vienne* were printed before 1501, one would almost have to suppose that an all-seeing fate intervened when each of the editions was almost lost and lent a special protection to the last survivor or two.

Originally, many more copies of *Paris et Vienne* must have been printed and sold than of the St. Ambrose *Opera*. The tremendously higher preservation rate of the latter is owing to the nature of its purchasers. Copies of the 1492 Ambrose went into established libraries where they might enjoy an undisturbed existence for generations on end. Probably the greatest single danger they had to face was the appearance of later collected editions of Ambrose, particularly those edited by Erasmus, which may have resulted in the replacement and eventual destruction of a number of copies of the outmoded original edition. When, in the late eighteenth and early nineteenth centuries, many of the European monasteries were secularized, their book collections were frequently transferred to a municipal, university, or state library or, if dispersed, went into the hands of a book trade which by then perceived medieval manuscripts and early printed books as having some market value and hence as worth preserving.

Again by contrast, the original owners of *Paris et Vienne* in its various early editions were mostly secular men and women who were in no position to preserve their books for futurity. They may not themselves have thought books of this kind worth special care once they and their friends and family had finished reading them. Numberless accidents and negligences over a few generations could easily result in the loss of all or virtually all copies of a given edition. Of such accidents are rarities born.

Broadside items such as indulgences have a particularly risky gauntlet to run if they are to survive at all. They would normally have been kept not in libraries or on bookshelves but in chests of family papers. Even there—unlike, for example, title deeds and other legal records, which were passed down from one generation to another—they would not have been thought of as papers to be permanently preserved. Their documentary value ended with the death of their purchasers, if not before. If the indulgence had been granted by a church which promised remembrance of the purchaser in its prayers, it would be sent back to the church on the owner's death, as a claim of spiritual benefits, and at that time its record value would cease. For all practical purposes, there were but two paths of survival open to indulgences. A copy executed and sold might remain more or less by accident in the papers of a family or a church, eventually perhaps coming to rest in a public archive. Or, a copy might reach the hands of a bookbinder and be preserved as endleaf, spine liner, or quire guard of a binding. More often than not, copies preserved as binding waste would have been leftover from the printing shop, that is, they would not have been executed copies, dated and containing the names of their purchasers. Such was the case with the copies in the Rosenwald Sammelband.

Some idea of the tremendous rate of loss of printed indulgences may be formed from several documentary references. Between 1498 and 1500, the great Benedictine convent of Montserrat, in Catalonia, commissioned the printing of more than 200,000 indulgences, some of which were printed in Barcelona, some at Montserrat itself. Of these 200,000, only 6 examples are known to have survived. Similarly, in 1500 the Bishop of Cefalù in Sicily paid a Messina printer for producing more than 130,000 indulgences and similar instruments. None of these are known to have survived.

Indulgence Printing in England

JUST AS INDULGENCES were among the earliest texts to be printed in Mainz, so was one among the earliest productions of William Caxton's Westminster printing shop. In 1928, a hitherto unrecorded indulgence printed with Caxton's types was discovered in the Public Record Office. This was an executed copy, which had been issued at Westminster on 13 December 1476 to Henry Langley and his wife Katherine. Caxton's shop must, therefore, have been in operation by that date. This is almost a year earlier than the next explicit date associated with Caxton's printing, the colophon date of 18 November 1477 in the *Dicts and Sayings of the Philosophers*, already mentioned above. Until recently, the 1476 indulgence was taken to be in fact the first piece of printing in England—a very modest cornerstone to what became a great edifice. It is now known that Caxton printed some five or six other books at Westminster in 1476, so the indulgence has lost its position of absolute primacy, but it remains a crucial document in the chronology of Caxton's printing career.

Although this sole surviving copy of the indulgence was sold on 13 December 1476, there is no particular reason to suppose that it had come fresh off the press that very day. It is more likely to have been printed at some earlier time. It was issued by virtue of Pope Sixtus IV's extension to England of the Jubilee indulgence he had awarded in 1475 to pilgrims visiting Rome. This special papal grant for England was made on or by 4 February 1476. Apparently, however, no collector of indulgence revenues was appointed until 24 May 1476, when John Sant, abbot of Abingdon, was named as papal commissary or collector of revenues. Allowing time for the appropriate documentation to reach England, and for the apparatus for collecting alms and issuing indulgences under its provisions to be set up, Caxton's indulgence forms would not have been printed off before the summer of 1476 at the earliest, even supposing that Abbot Sant had immediately decided to take advantage of the newly founded printing press for multiplying copies. In fact, a number of manuscript copies of Sant's indulgence survive from 1476 and 1477, so it is evident that Caxton's press was not entirely relied on for the production of indulgence forms. Like the 1475 Rome Jubilee indulgence on which it was based, the 1476 Jubilee indulgence for England was intended to raise money for a Christian fleet in the eastern Mediterranean, to counter the Turkish advance. The papal camera eventually received about eight thousand florins from English sales of this indulgence.

The next record of indulgence printing in England comes in 1480, when funds were solicited to support the Knights Hospitallers in their defense of the island of Rhodes against Turkish siege. This indulgence campaign was authorized by Sixtus IV on 12 December 1479, and it was to remain valid for just over a year, from Palm Sunday, 26 March 1480, to Easter Day, 22 April 1481. The commissary for this indulgence was John Kendale, the highest-ranking Englishman in the military-religious order of the Knights Hospitallers, or Knights of St. John of Rhodes. Kendale must have made immediate arrangements with Caxton to get printed indulgence forms ready at the beginning of the campaign, for the only surviving copy of Caxton's first printing of the indulgence was sold to Simon and Emma Mountfort on 31 March 1480, just five days after Palm Sunday.

The Rhodes indulgence campaign of 1480–81 was not restricted to England. Well over two dozen printed editions of indulgence documents related to it survive from the Continent, issued by various commissaries in the Low Countries, the German states, and the Swiss confederation. The campaign was certainly successful in England. Caxton eventually printed at least two more editions of the 1480 Rhodes indulgence. John Lettou, who had recently set up a printing shop in London after migrating from Rome, printed at least three. These six printings would have produced some thousands of copies, but they survive today in a total of just nine copies, most of which are fragmented binder's waste. In fact, if the fragments from bindings are put aside, we should know of the existence of only two printings of the Rhodes indulgence.

The name of the Hospitaller who issued the Rhodes indulgences just mentioned, John Kendale, should ring familiar to the attentive reader, for it has already been quoted a few pages back, from the beginning lines of the St. Mary of Rounceval indulgence. This suggests a connection between the Rhodes and Rounceval indulgences that is well worth pursuing. The circumstances leading to the printing of the Rounceval indulgence, its purpose, and the way in which it was distributed will become more vivid when considered in relation to the history of St. Mary of Rounceval.

The Hospital of St. Mary Rounceval

OUR LADY OF ROUNCEVAL was founded in the village of Charing, between the City of London and Westminster, in the early thirteenth century. As its name indicates, it was an offshoot of the priory of Roncesvalles in Navarre, a conventual hospital of widespread fame for its protection and charity to the many travelers who passed by it on the road between France and Spain—and especially to the pilgrims going to the shrine of St. James at Compostella. The first great patron of the London hospital, and almost certainly its founder, was William Marshal, second earl of Pembroke, son of the more famous William Marshal who served as regent of England after the death of King John in 1216. The hospital was built on lands given by the younger William Marshal, who also endowed it with properties elsewhere in England and Wales. The grounds of St. Mary Rounceval fronted on the Thames, where Charing Cross Station now stands—the Embankment, claiming additional dry land from the north bend of the river here, lay centuries off in the future. Inland, the hospital precincts bordered the Strand, the heavily trafficked road connecting Westminster to the City of London proper. The hospital was responsible for keeping the road in good repair at this point.

A medieval hospital, it should be said, was a very different thing from the modern conception of a hospital. It was an ecclesiastical institution, existing to aid the sick and the needy in response to the religious doctrine of charity as a good work. Its aim was to care for rather than cure its inmates, and the central object of its care was the soul, not the body. Accordingly, the nucleus of a hospital was its chapel, and a chief concern of its rules was the maintenance of religious services. Many hospitals were administered directly by monasteries and almost all organized themselves according to a monastic or quasi-monastic rule, most commonly the Augustinian rule. Several established orders of the Church had a particular

FIG. 8 Detail from Anthonis van den Wyngaerde's panorama of London, ca. 1545, showing Westminster to Charing Cross. The buildings of the hospital of St. Mary Rounceval are probably those lying directly between Charing Cross and the Thames.

duty to operate hospitals—the orders of St. Lazarus of Jerusalem, St. Mary of Bethlehem (the London house of which, by long tradition a refuge for the insane, has given us the word *bedlam*), and others. St. Mary Rounceval seems to have been the only long-continuing English cell of the priory of Roncesvalles in Navarre, though a second Roncesvalles cell may have had a brief existence in Norwich in the 1360s.

The number of medieval English hospitals was always in flux, for they were often rather small and insecurely financed corporations, which in the absence of special patronage might decay or be refounded to other purposes. Many seem to have gone under in the 1340s, at the time of the Black Plague. But new foundations came into existence more or less steadily in the later Middle Ages, and at any time between the thirteenth century and the monastic dissolutions of Henry VIII there would have been perhaps five hundred or so hospitals active in England. A few of these of special reputation, such as St. Bartholomew's or St. Thomas of Acon in London, had very substantial incomes, as great as those of some of the cathedral churches and greater than all but a few of the Oxford and Cambridge colleges. St. Mary

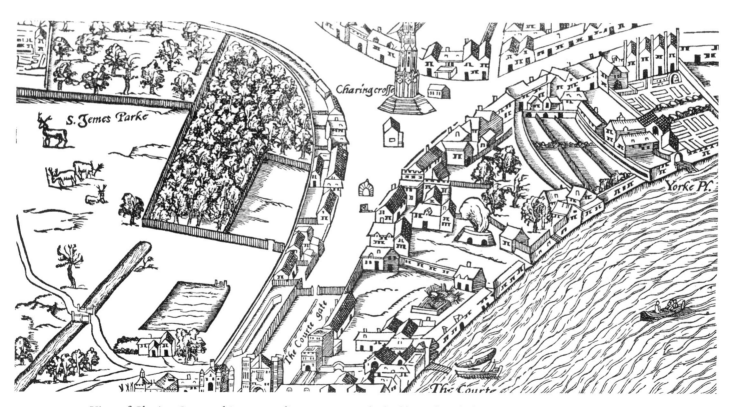

FIG. 9 View of Charing Cross and its surroundings, ca. 1562. The buildings directly between Charing Cross and the Thames are likely to be the former hospital of St. Mary Rounceval.

Rounceval stood at a lower level, not nearly so wealthy as these. As we shall shortly see, however, it had its own special reputation in the fourteenth century, though rather an unsavory one.

There is not space here to summarize all the thirteenth- to sixteenth-century documentary records that concern Our Lady of Rounceval. But several events in the hospital's history must be mentioned as they bear more or less directly on the Rosenwald indulgence. In 1385, a guild or fraternity was founded at the hospital, for the special purpose of celebrating the feast of the nativity of the Virgin, 8 September; the guild paid for a special mass on that day. Guilds of this kind existed by the hundreds in late medieval England. Guild organizations may, without exaggeration, be claimed as the most pervasive and most characteristic form of social bond in the fourteenth and fifteenth centuries, outside of the family itself. Throughout England, in cities, towns, and rural parishes, men and women created and joined guilds from a combination of religious and social motives.

There is a tendency today to think of guilds as primarily economic associations, whose purpose was to control the operations of crafts and trades in a given town by restricting their practice to sworn guild members. Guilds of this type did develop, including, conspicuously, the great merchant guilds of London, Bristol, and several other towns. Nonetheless, these were only the tip of the iceberg. The great majority of the guilds had simpler and more centrally religious purposes. The defining feature of all guilds was that they were attached to specific churches or chapels and took on themselves the duty of helping to maintain services there—ambitiously, perhaps, by supporting a chantry priest, or humbly, by keeping a candle burning. Other usual obligations of guild membership might be to keep friendship with one another, to see deceased members decently buried, to distribute alms and bread to the needy. Members sometimes, for greater fellowship, agreed to dress in common suit, and that is how Chaucer in the Prologue to *Canterbury Tales* presents a group of notably prosperous guildsmen:

> An haberdassher and a carpenter
> A webbe, a dyere, and a tapicer,
> Were with us eek, clothed in o*on* liveree
> Of a solempne and greet fraternitee
> [*webbe*: weaver; *tapicer*: upholsterer]

From the late 1370s onward, control of the hospital of St. Mary Rounceval was at issue between the parent house of Roncesvalles and the English Crown. This controversy was part of a broader movement of the 1370s, when the wars with France intensified the traditional English xenophobia and led to the suppression of many "alien priories"—religious houses affiliated to continental monasteries. In 1389 the warden of the hospital was a canon named Garcias, who clearly had been sent out from Navarre. But he was probably the last foreign-born warden, all his known successors being native Englishmen who received Crown appointments. In 1393, for example, the warden of Rounceval was John Gedney, who shortly before had displaced Geoffrey Chaucer from a well-paid situation as clerk of the king's works. But even after the 1390s, Our Lady of Rounceval maintained some ties with Roncesvalles. In 1432 Henry VI permitted alms collected by the hospital to be sent out of the country to Navarre, and one hundred years later the hospital was still remitting ten marks per year to its parent house. Our Lady of Rounceval was apparently financially distressed in the early 1420s when the vicar of St. Martin's in the Fields, which lay close by, complained that the hospital was detaining his tithes, under the supposed authority of letters of Boniface IX and other popes. The archbishop of Canterbury seized these letters and sent them to Rome, where the papal chancery declared them forgeries.

In 1475, King Edward IV granted a patent to a guild or fraternity at Rounceval which was to maintain a perpetual chantry of one priest who would pray for the king and his family as well as for the men and women of the guild. It is not certain whether this is, in uninterrupted succession, the same guild as had existed in the fourteenth century or whether the hospital had decayed of recent years and a new guild was founded there as part of a renovation. In any event, three years later Edward granted the hospital and all its properties (which presumably had been in Crown hands for some decades) to the guild, which undertook to maintain three chaplains and give aid as by tradition to the poor people visiting its infirmary.

The warden of the hospital is not named in these documents, but he was probably the man whom, by testimony of the Rosenwald indulgence, we know to have been warden a few years later: Edward Poynings. Poynings was a well-born and well-connected canon lawyer, educated at Winchester School, Oxford, and Cambridge. He was the son of a baron, and the uncle of Sir Edward Poynings, who a few years hence rose in rebellion against Richard III, became a mainstay of the Tudor house, and served as lord deputy of Ireland. Our Edward Poynings seems to have led a comfortable clerical existence, contributing nothing notable to his church or to learning, but gathering into his hands in the course of time a number of well-paying benefices.

Indulgences Issued by St. Mary Rounceval

IT IS, in a sense, historically just that an indulgence issued by Our Lady of Rounceval should finally have come to light; for there is reason to believe that in the mind of a late-medieval Everyman, the name of Rounceval would have been immediately and inextricably associated with the idea of indulgences and their abuse. The locus classicus for this image of

A bokeler hadde he maad hym of a Cake
With hym ther rood a gentil pardoner
Of rouncyuale his freend & his comper
That streight was come fro the court of Rome
Ful lowde he song com hidir lene grom
This somprour baar to hym a styf burdon
Was neuer trompe of half so greet a soun
This pardoner hadde heer as yelow as wex
And smothe it hyng as doth a strike of flex
By hounces hyng his lockis that he hadde
And ther with his sholdris ouer spradde
But than it lay be Culpons one and one
An hood for cold wered he none
For it was trussed vp on his walet
Hym thoughte he rood vp on the newe get
Disshupld saue his cappe he rood albare
Suche glarynge yen hadde he as hath an hare
His walet beforn hym had he in his lappe
A vernacle hadde he sowid vp on his cappe
Brette ful of pardon com fro Rome al hoot
A vois he hadde as smal as hath a goot
No berd hadde he ne neuer sholde haue
As moche was it as it were newe shaue
I trowe he were a geldyng or a mare
But of his craft from Berwik vnto Ware
Ne was ther nowher suche a pardoner
For in his male he hadde a pilow beer
Whiche that he sayde was our ladies veyll
He sayde he hadde a gobet of the seyll

FIG. 10 The description of the Pardoner from the first edition of Geoffrey Chaucer, *The Canterbury Tales* [1477].

Rounceval is the *Canterbury Tales*, where the company traveling to St. Thomas à Becket's shrine included "a gentil Pardoner of Rouncival," a distinctly unedifying creature whose pride in his long yellow locks was such that he could not bear to cover them with his hood, and who in other ways struck Chaucer as less than fully masculine:

> No berd hadde he, ne never sholde have,
> As smooth it was as it were late y-shave;
> I trowe he were a gelding or a mare.

But as to this insinuation, it should in justice be added that the Pardoner himself claimed to possess "a joly wenche in every toun." His wallet was "bret-ful of pardoun come from Rome al hoot," and he told the company with great frankness that he would collect money for his pardons from anyone, no matter what hardship this might inflict:

> Al were it yeven of the povrest page,
> Or of the povrest widwe in a village,
> Al sholde hir children sterve for famyne.

We may accept that in specifying the Pardoner as an agent of the hospital of Rounceval, Chaucer was supplying detail of a kind intended to strike his audience as appropriate and characteristic. In the satirical poem of *Friar Daw Topias*, about a decade later than this, the pardoner of Rounceval again stands as one of the types of his breed:

> I trowe thou menys the pardonystres
> Of Seint Thomas of Acres,
> Of Antoun, or of Rouncevale,
> That rennen so fast aboute.

The privilege of granting indulgences or pardons was, in the Middle Ages, delegated by the pope and by bishops at various times to hundreds of religious entities. Hospitals and guilds, which stood practically at the bottom of the ecclesiastical hierarchy, were especially dependent on funds raised through this channel. A large part of their revenues came from alms rather than from rentals of property or, as in the case of parish churches, from tithes. Some portion of alms could be collected casually from poor boxes and the like, but to find substantial donations, and especially donations from outside of the immediate neighborhood, a hospital (let us say) would have to offer in return some recognized benefit. The hospital which could repay a gift of alms—an act of charity by Catholic doctrine—by the grant of an indulgence was much more strongly situated than one lacking this privilege.

By the conceptions of church law an indulgence was not sold but freely granted. Its recipient did not buy it but rather, by performing a work of mercy through almsgiving, showed that he was worthy of it. Likewise, a pardoner (to give him his common English name) could not according to the laws of the church give pardon or absolution. The receiver

¶ The tale of the Pardoner

For though my self be a ful vicious man
A moralle tale yet I you telle can
Whiche I am wont for to preche and also wynne
Now holde your pees my tale I wol begynne

¶ Here endyth the prologue
Of the Pardoner

¶ And begynneth the Tale

IN flaundris sumtyme was a companye
Of yonge folke that hauntedyn folye
As ryot hazard Stewys and tauarnys
Where as wyth harpes lutes and gyternes
They daunce and pleye at the dyce both day & nyght
And etyn also & drynkyn aboue her myght
Thorow whiche they doon the deuyl sacrifise

FIG. 11 Woodcut of the Pardoner from the second edition of Geoffrey Chaucer, *The Canterbury Tales* [1483].

of an indulgence had to be—as the formulas of indulgences, including that of the Rosenwald indulgence, always state—truly contrite and properly confessed, whereupon his confessor could release him from various penances according to the terms of the indulgence. This was theory. But books could be filled, and have been, with evidences that the reality was different. From the thirteenth century onward, throughout Europe, there is ample testimony that pardoners regularly misrepresented their office and powers in their quest for alms. This testimony comes not only from opponents of the established church, such as Wycliffe and his heirs, but also from a multitude of papal and conciliar legislation and reports. As a result, in English records, both literary and documentary, the name of pardoner has appeared much more frequently in negative contexts than in neutral or positive ones. At best, it is a word, like *dogcatcher*, that can mean nothing very inspiring. In the numerous and popular fifteenth-century lists of "company terms," where group nouns such as "covey of quail," "brace of hounds," and "pride of lions" were collected for amusement, we find always a "lying of pardoners."

FIG. 12   Seal of the hospital of
St. Mary Rounceval, Charing Cross.
A seal of this type would have been attached
to the Rounceval letters of confraternity.

The commonest form of indulgence instrument issued by hospitals and guilds was the letter of fraternity or confraternity, and this is the form exemplified in the Rounceval indulgence. It is different in kind from the earlier indulgences printed by Caxton, in 1476 and 1480, which simply recited the benefits granted by the pope in return for gifts aiding the fight against the Turks. A letter of fraternity enrolled its bearer in all the spiritual benefits enjoyed by members of the fraternity. In particular, the bearer would be included, after his or her death, in the intercessory prayers of the guild, which would, in theory, continue into

perpetuity. Just such benefits were promised by the Rounceval indulgence, whose text is
given here in translation:

> Edward Ponyngs, chaplain of the lord king, master or keeper of the hospital of the
> blessed and glorious virgin Mary of Rounceval, at Charing Cross outside of the walls of
> London; John Kendale, valet of the crown of the said lord king, and John Lynton, proc-
> tors general of the fraternity or guild in honor of the said blessed and glorious virgin
> Mary, founded and established in the aforesaid chapel or hospital: to our beloved in
> Christ [space for names], greetings, and may eternal grace attend you. From the testimony
> of the Sacred Word, we learn that the more copiously spiritual goods are distributed to
> Christ's worshipers, so much the more abundantly do the worshipers, through their acts
> of piety, receive and take on grace. Therefore, learning of the strength of your devotion
> to our hospital, to which you are most sincerely moved by the urgings of charity out of
> your reverence for God and for the glorious virgin Mary His mother; and wishing more-
> over to give you in return some godly reward; by these presents we make you partic-
> ipants in all the spiritual goods, as well in life as after death, which our brethren and sisters
> now or ever shall enjoy through the clemency of Our Savior. Namely, of all masses,
> prayers, fasts, vigils, pilgrimages to the Holy Land, consecrated with Christ's blood, and
> to the city of Rome, dyed with the blood of the holy apostles and martyrs. Whereas Pope
> Clement VI by his special grace granted to all those, truly confessed and contrite of their
> sins, who shall in charity have given or assigned in any way some part of their goods to
> the said hospital, its master and brethren, or who shall have enrolled themselves in its
> confraternity, a reduction of one-third of the penance required of them, and an indul-
> gence of three years and one hundred days; and whereas many other of the Roman pon-
> tiffs have, by their mercy, together with Pope Clement, granted to the benefactors of the
> aforesaid hospital, full participation in all the spiritual aids which are or shall be in the
> universal church, and a thousand [text lacking] . . . and by the most holy [pope Clement
> it is granted that you may choose a suitable confessor, and he may] as it pleases him re-
> lease [you from your vows], and by his mercy let them be exchanged for lighter ones,
> always excepting vows of pilgrimage to Jerusalem and Rome, of entering holy orders,
> and of chastity; and by his special grace [Clement has] added that when, by the presenta-
> tion of these presents, your deaths are announced in the aforesaid chapel or hospital,
> the same shall be done for you as is done for our deceased brethren and sisters, friends
> and benefactors, by common custom. In testimony of which matters the seal of the
> aforesaid proctors general is attached to these presents. Given in the hospital [of St.
> Mary Rounceval, on a certain date].

The indulgence fragments preserved in the Rosenwald Sammelband are representative
of countless thousands of long-vanished indulgence letters issued by the hospital of Rounceval
over several centuries. The Rounceval indulgence names, as earliest guarantor of the spiritual
benefits it grants, Clement VI, one of the Avignonese popes (1342–52). We may suppose

with good likelihood that Clement's indulgence grant was made to the Navarre priory of Roncesvalles, and extended by them to their London cell. Slightly later in the fourteenth century, but still earlier than Chaucer's reference to the Rounceval pardoner, we know that the hospital was actively raising moneys by means of indulgence sales. In 1372 John of Gaunt, duke of Lancaster, addressed letters to several ecclesiastics, powerfully requesting them to aid the hospital's proctors in their alms collections. John of Gaunt's London residence, the Savoy Inn, was a near neighbor of the hospital, and the duke may well have worshiped in the Rounceval chapel.

John of Gaunt's letters of patronage for Rounceval were written because, though the rule was often breached, pardoners needed permission from bishops before entering their dioceses to collect alms. Because of this rule it was known, even before the Rosenwald indulgence came to light, that the proctors of Our Lady of Rounceval were busy about their tasks of money-gathering in the late fifteenth and early sixteenth centuries. Episcopal registers from this time record entry permits allowing the Rounceval proctors to operate, for instance, in the diocese of Hereford. Just such indulgence forms as the one printed by Caxton would have been in their baggage. Pardoners advertised their wares most commonly by addresses to parish congregations, and it may well be imagined that curates would not welcome the sight of scarce alms being alienated into the hands of strangers. The clergy could not deny venue to a properly licensed pardoner, nor were they permitted to take payments from the pardoners. But the latter regulation was continually violated. Parochial accounts not infrequently include receipts of payments from pardoners, and the accounts of a church in Chester, in the mid-1530s, specify that one such payment was made by a pardoner of Rounceval. Elsewhere in England, we know that the clergy sometimes pursued their claims to such donatives in the church courts, as a matter of customary right.

It is not difficult to imagine, in rough outline, the circumstances that would have led to Caxton's printing indulgence forms for Our Lady of Rounceval. One of the hospital's two proctors was John Kendale, who was already in 1480 chiefly responsible for indulgence sales in England on behalf of the Knights Hospitallers or Knights of Rhodes. The central house of the Hospitallers was in the suburbs of London, at Clerkenwell, but Kendale's business must have taken him often enough to the courts of Westminster. In 1480 Kendale and Caxton were joint witnesses when the churchwarden's accounts in the church of St. Margaret's, Westminster, were proved. It may be noted that one of the chaplains supported by the guild of Our Lady of Rounceval served an altar at St. Margaret's.

The connection of Kendale with the Rounceval indulgence suggests 1480 as its likeliest year of issue, for it is only in that year that we have record of Kendale's activity in the sale of indulgences. The Rounceval indulgences may well have been distributed together with the Rhodes indulgences, as a kind of minor pendant—a favor to the Rounceval guild on Kendale's part—to the Rhodes campaign; for pardoners did not necessarily deal in only one type of

FIG. 13   Portrait medal of John Kendale, 1480, attributed to Niccolo Fiorentino. The reverse displays Kendale's arms.

indulgence. In fact, because it was not practical for every hospital or guild issuing indulgences to maintain a cadre of proctors all over England, the sale of pardons was regularly farmed out to local collectors, who would return fixed, agreed sums each year to the hospitals or guilds they served, in return for the privilege of selling their indulgences within a county or group of counties.

We do not know whether the hospital of Rounceval was resorting to this shift in the early 1480s, at the time of Caxton's indulgence, but it certainly did so in the 1520s. Scattered accounts of the hospital survive from this time, listing the names of the local pardoners or proctors, the moneys received, and the regions for which they were responsible. The same accounts show that indulgence forms and bills advertising indulgences continued to be printed for the hospital of Rounceval by Wynkyn de Worde, who in the early 1490s succeeded to Caxton's printing and publishing business, and by Robert Copland who, like Wynkyn, formerly worked in Caxton's shop. Thus, in the hospital records from Michaelmas (29 September) 1520 to Michaelmas 1521, we find a payment

> to Mr Wylkyns the prynter for CC breves to sett vppon the Churche dores at viij d. the C summa   xvj d.

followed by another payment

> for past for breves agaynst the visitacion of our lady   ob.

Which is to say that Wynkyn ("Wylkyns") was paid 16 pence for printing 200 briefs, or indulgence bills, at the rate of 8 pence per 100; and that another halfpenny was laid out for the paste for putting them up on the doors of London's churches at the feast of the Visitation, 2 July. Later in the summer of 1521 Wynkyn was paid at the same rate to print 300 more such bills, and another halfpenny's worth of paste was spent for placarding them at Assumptiontide, 15 August, and the same again at the Nativity of Our Lady, 8 September. In the accounts for 1523–24, Robert Copland was paid a sum of 7 shillings 6 pence for printing 500 letters of indulgence, a rate of 18 pence per 100 forms. These chance documentary references imply that during the decades of the late fifteenth and early sixteenth centuries the hospital of Rounceval commissioned the printing of many thousands of such indulgence forms and advertisements, instruments that earlier would each have had to be written out by hand. Of these thousands, the vellum strips in the Rosenwald Sammelband are the solitary survival.

The Rounceval indulgence in the Library of Congress is the earliest printed letter of confraternity to survive from England. The next one after it was also printed by Caxton, in 1485, on behalf of the Dominican priory in Arundel, Surrey. It, too, is a recent discovery, found in England among family papers deposited in a county record office; it has not yet been published. The other surviving printed letters of confraternity belong to the early sixteenth century. They number in the dozens and were issued by a wide assortment of hospitals and guilds. As has already been suggested and as the records of the hospital of Rounceval further emphasize, these surviving indulgence forms can be only the most minute fraction of those once issued.

It is noteworthy, and surely significant, that very few printed letters of confraternity or other indulgence instruments are known later than about 1530, for the traditional patterns of English religious life were under severe stress at this time and were soon to be shattered. Indulgences were but one element in the complex tissue of late medieval piety, other components of which included the cults of relics and of local saints; pilgrimages; fear of the torments of purgatory, and belief in the intercessory powers of saints to relieve or release from these torments; and a taste for edifying tales involving visions, miraculous interventions in everyday life, the magical virtues of the sacramental wafer. From its beginnings, the printing press in England served the needs and tastes of this simple and credulous piety not only with indulgences but also with such collections of saints' lives and other religious stories as the *Golden Legend* translated by Caxton, John Mirk's *Festial*, and many smaller devotional tracts. In his own life, Caxton was, by all evidence, a fair representative of this brand of lay piety.

By the fourth decade of the sixteenth century, England's traditional religious practices were under attack from many quarters. Several strands of opposition were ingrained and ancient. First, alongside and often intermingled in the spirit of simple piety, there had long existed a strong anticlerical strain in English society which, though perhaps not questioning the church's doctrine, nevertheless regarded the ecclesiastical establishment with cynicism, finding in it many evidences of slackness, venality, and corruption. A more active challenge to the establishment came from the Lollard heresy, whose doctrine was formed by the banned writings of the Oxford theologian John Wycliffe (d. 1384) and his followers. Wycliffe had attacked on doctrinal grounds such aspects of Catholic religious life as devotion to saints, pilgrimages, and indulgences. Though rigorously suppressed, Lollardy was never extinguished, and there are signs that from the end of the fifteenth century onward it was enjoying a rebirth.

In the second and third decades of the sixteenth century, these native strands of anti-clericalism and Lollardy were corroborated by new continental ideas of reform. The Christian humanism of Erasmus, though never unorthodox, found much to mock in such credulous practices as the cult of relics and emphasized the lack of scriptural authority for this and many other traditional pious exercises. Martin Luther's outpouring of writings, which was in fact first triggered by disgust at the abuse of indulgences, directly challenged the papal authority. Finally, it was around this time that "the king's great matter," Henry VIII's determination to divorce Catherine of Aragon and marry Anne Boleyn, was reaching a stage of crisis that would soon sever England entirely from communion with the church of Rome—not from any doctrinal quarrel, for Henry considered himself purely orthodox, but simply to satisfy the royal will.

In the mid-1530s, Henry ordered the dissolution of the monasteries and seizure of their lands. Smaller religious corporations came under attack in the next years, including many of the hospitals. Finally, shortly after Henry VIII's death in 1547, the first parliament of his still-minor son, Edward VI, ordered the dissolution of all chantries, colleges of priests, hospitals, guilds, and fraternities, in consequence of their "devising and phantasying vain opinions of purgatory and masses satisfactory, to be done for them which be departed." Here, for the first time, specific Protestant doctrine was used to justify the seizures.

The experience of Rounceval during the years after 1530 was probably typical of many other small religious foundations. The hospital continued to operate through the 1530s, for we know that as late as 1537 its pardoners were still plying their trade through the English countryside, but revenues fell off considerably. In 1520 the Rounceval pardoners had collected revenues of about twenty pounds, and the subscription payments of guild members brought in another ten pounds. By 1539 receipts from the pardoners seem to have ceased, and payments from guild members had declined to little more than three pounds. By this time the hospital must have been breaking up, though it is not certain when it stopped giving shelter to the sick. Henry VIII took a forced loan of forty-three pounds from the hospital's endowment, which (it scarcely needs saying) was never repaid. In 1541 the tabernacle from the chapel of Rounceval was set up in the Trinity chapel of St. Margaret's, Westminster, and we may take it that by that time the hospital had ceased to function. In November 1544 the hospital of Rounceval formally surrendered itself into royal hands. In Edward VI's reign, the property of Rounceval was leased to the master of revels, Sir Thomas Cawarden. By 1600, its buildings were in the hands of the earl of Northampton, who tore them down to supply material for his new London residence.

The Rosenwald Sammelband Revisited

ONE CHIEF QUESTION concerning the Rosenwald Sammelband has still not been encountered. It was stated briefly above that the binding of this volume was some fifty or sixty years later than the dates of the four Caxton editions it comprises. How, one may properly wonder, did a bindery of this period, the fourth decade of the sixteenth century, happen to have printed vellum waste from half a century before—the Rounceval indulgences —lying about the place? Is it only coincidence that the binding joins together four Caxton folios printed 1479–81 and indulgence forms printed by Caxton about 1480?

The shop producing the binding can be identified: it was that of John Reynes, a prominent London bookseller and publisher. Reynes was originally a native of Guelders in the Low Countries, and he was granted letters of denizenship in London in 1510. At least five hundred bindings survive from Reynes's shop in St. Paul's churchyard, more than from any other bindery of Tudor England. With one or two exceptions, they are all of simple blind-tooled calf, reflecting Reynes's extensive retail trade in ready-bound books; the decoration of his bindings was rarely elaborate. Reynes owned about ten pictorial panel stamps, which were impressed into the covers of bindings by means of a screw press. The illustrations on the panels include the arms of England and other Tudor emblems, and St. George slaying the dragon—Reynes's shop being located under the sign of St. George. His bindery also possessed a few pictorial rolls and a handful of rather nondescript smaller tools of the type commonly referred to as "pineapple" (meaning, at this time, pinecone) stamps. One of Reynes's rolls and several of his panel stamps incorporated his cipher, by which means they can be unambiguously identified as his.

The layout of the tooling on the Rosenwald volume is wholly characteristic of Reynes's work, or rather of his binders' work, for we may assume that Reynes was, at least in his prime years, too successfully active as bookseller and publisher to spend his time at the manual labor of binding. A roll historiated with a bee, bird, hound, thistle, flowers, and Reynes's cipher is used to mark out a central panel on each cover. The panels are divided by fillets into a diamond or diaper pattern, the compartments of which are impressed with Reynes's pineapple stamps. Reynes seems to have acquired this particular roll around 1520, so from the tooling alone the binding might date to anytime between then and Reynes's death in early 1544. Printed waste in the covers helps narrow the interval. The inside of each cover is lined with a blank paper leaf, covering the turn-ins of the leather. Beneath each blank leaf is a printed leaf. These two printed leaves belong to a folio edition of Pliny, *Historia naturalis*, published by Hieronymus Froben in Basel, 1530. Reynes's binding must therefore be later than 1530. Since it is not likely that leaves of Froben's edition (which Reynes would have

FIG. 14   A London binding by John Reynes, ca. 1535, covers the Rosenwald Sammelband.

FIG. 15   Rubricated initials in the Rosenwald Sammelband.

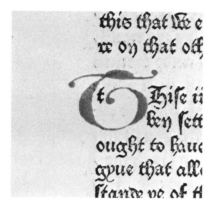

acquired for retail) were immediately used as binder's waste, the Rosenwald binding is probably some few years later, ca. 1535–40 being a reasonable approximate date.

What, then, of the four or more Caxton-printed indulgences, ca. 1480, used as quire guards in this volume? Their existence makes sense only when it is understood that the four Caxton editions making up the volume had been together long before they were bound by Reynes. All four texts contain rubrication—red-ink initial letters and paragraphing marks—drawn by a single hand, a hand obviously much earlier than the mid-1530s and closely related, for example, to the rubrications found in most of the surviving copies of Caxton's 1482 edition of the *Polycronicon*. These rubrications would have been written in before binding, when the four copies were still in sheets. Moreover, one of the four texts, *Dicts of the Philosophers*, contains red-ink quiring. That is, the sheets of each quire were numbered by hand, in the lower right corner, to show the sequence in which they were to be gathered together. The first and third texts, *Mirror of the World* and *Cicero*, already had printed quiring and so did not need manuscript quiring to be added; and the fourth text, *Cordiale*, shows no signs of manuscript quiring.

FIG. 16 Lower cover of a volume bound in Caxton's bindery, ca. 1486. The volume originally contained as pastedowns two copies of an indulgence printed by Caxton in 1481.

When it is considered that the four Caxton editions in the volume were first issued within a two-and-a-half-year span, 1479–81; that they were rubricated by a single hand, little if any later than that time; and that their quires were guarded with strips of multiple unused copies of a Caxton-printed indulgence, itself probably dating to 1480—when these various facts are put together, their combined implication is that long before the Reynes binding took its place, these four copies must by all probability have been joined in a binding from Caxton's bindery.

It has long been recognized that a Westminster bindery was closely associated with Caxton's printing and publishing business. About three dozen bindings from this shop have been recorded, interconnected by their use of a common group of decorative tools. About half these bindings cover books printed either by Caxton or by his successor Wynkyn de Worde. A number of others are on manuscripts written or used in the Westminster precincts. Most of the remainder are on continental printed books that could plausibly have been sold by Caxton or Wynkyn as part of their broader bookselling activities. The identity of the binder or binders of these books, who must have been active, whether singly or in succession, from the late 1470s to 1511 or so, is not known. It is very probable, though not entirely certain, that this bindery worked directly for Caxton, that is, formed part of his book business. There is no evidence for the bindery's activity before Caxton set up in Westminster in 1476. Moreover, the tools and layout of many of the bindings, particularly of the early ones, closely resemble those of Bruges bookbindings. Caxton, it will be recalled, had printed for several years in Bruges before transferring his activities to England.

The connection of this bindery with Caxton is suggested not only by the large number of its bindings covering his books but also by the number of its bindings containing printed waste from his shop. At least nine of the volumes from Caxton's bindery (as we may call it) contain printed fragments from Caxton's or, in one case, Wynkyn's shop. Some half-dozen pieces of printing by Caxton, including two indulgences of 1481, would have disappeared without record except for this fortuitous preservation. To this group must now be added the Rounceval indulgence.

Every old book, like the notorious penny passed from hand to hand, has its own tale to tell. The tale of the Rosenwald Sammelband, so far as we can reconstruct it, is as follows. Sometime in the early 1480s, but not before the closing months of 1481, a customer visited Caxton's shop at Westminster, near the chapter house of the abbey. He (or she) selected four folio editions and placed an order for them to be bound together. The customer wanted some extra finish to be given to the books, in the form of professional rubrications, and this requirement Caxton was able to supply. A rubricator was set to work on the sheets, and it was probably at this time, too, that one of the texts was quired in red (at least two other volumes from Caxton's bindery, in the Morgan Library, also contain red-ink quiring). After the rubrications were added, the volume was assembled, sewn, and put into leather-covered boards. Among the bits and pieces of vellum scrap in the bindery, laid by for the needful hour, were leftover copies of the confraternity letters that Caxton had printed recently for the neighboring hospital of St. Mary Rounceval, by Charing Cross—binders are like pack rats in hoarding such things. A sheaf of these was put to good service, being cut into strips to reinforce the quire folds against the pull of the thread. Eventually the volume was ready, and the customer took delivery.

Some fifty or sixty years later, the volume needed repairs. This is perhaps the most surprising aspect of its history, for the binding given it in Caxton's shop would have been a sturdy construction, proof against normal battering. Whatever the cause of its dilapidation by the 1530s, the book had probably not moved far, for it was given to the bindery of a London bookseller, John Reynes, for reparations. It is likely that the Caxton volume was now entirely resewn, and that at this time most of the vellum quire guards were lost. Reynes's bindery also kept miscellaneous scraps around, among which were sheets of the 1530 Basel edition of Pliny's *Natural History*. Two leaves of this waste were pasted into the book, one on the inside of each cover, and white paper was laid over these. Conceivably, the Caxton volume was by now an article of secondhand commerce, which had come to Reynes and which he thought worth refurbishing. In any case, a contents note in a clear, professional hand was added to the inside of the front cover about this time.

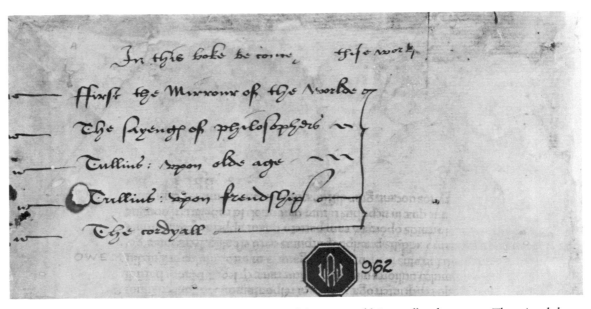

FIG. 17   Contents note written on the front pastedown of the Rosenwald Sammelband, ca. 1535. The printed show-through is a wasteleaf from Pliny, *Historia naturalis* (Basel, 1530), used to line the inside of the board.

For the next three hundred-odd years the volume's history is obscure. It made its way somehow to that "old Manor House in the North" from which it reemerged in the early twentieth century. A dozen generations of anonymous owners had managed to keep it safe from fire, water, insects, and rodent's tooth until it was called to the auction block. It soon afterward crossed the Atlantic to America, and passed through several private collections until it reached the hands of Lessing J. Rosenwald, by whose philanthropy it has become part of our public treasure.

Abbreviations

Bdr's Waste	Material itemized in Appendix C.
Blades	*The Life and Typography of William Caxton*, by William Blades. 2 vols. London, 1861–63. (Numbers cited in parentheses refer to the abridgment, *The Biography and Typography of William Caxton*, London, 1877).
Blake	*Caxton's Own Prose*, ed. N. F. Blake. London, 1973.
BMC	*Catalogue of Books Printed in the XVth Century Now in the British Museum*. 10 vols. London, 1908–71.
CA	*Annales de la typographie néerlandaise du XVe siècle*, by M. F. A. G. Campbell. The Hague, 1874. And *1er [–4e] Supplément*. The Hague, 1878–90.
Claudin	*Histoire de l'imprimerie en France au XVe siècle*, by Anatole Claudin. 4 vols. (uncompleted). Paris, 1900–1914.
Cop.	W. A. Copinger. *Supplement to Hain's Repertorium bibliographicum*. 3 vols. London, 1895–1902.
Cx	Material itemized in Appendix D.
Delisle	Chantilly, [Musée Condé], Cabinet des Livres. *Imprimés antérieurs au milieu du XVIe siècle*, ed. Leopold Delisle. Paris, 1905.
DeR	*A Census of Caxtons*, by Seymour De Ricci. Oxford, 1909.
Duff	*Fifteenth Century English Books*, by E. Gordon Duff. Oxford, 1917.
Einbl.	*Einblattdrucke des XV. Jahrhunderts* . . . herausgegeben von der Kommission für den Gesamtkatalog der Wiegendrucke. Halle a.S., 1914.
Goff	*Incunabula in American Libraries, a Third Census*, by Frederick R. Goff. New York, 1964. And *Supplement*. New York, 1972.
GW	*Gesamtkatalog der Wiegendrucke*. 8(+) vols. Leipzig, 1925–38; Stuttgart (etc.), 1978– .
Hain	*Repertorium bibliographicum, in quo libri omnes ab arte typographica inventa usque ad annum MD. enumerantur*, by Ludwig Hain. 2 vols. (in 4). Stuttgart (etc.), 1826–38.
Mead	*Incunabula in the Huntington Library*, by Herman R. Mead. San Marino, Calif., 1937.
Mellon	*Fifty-five Books Printed before 1525* . . . *An Exhibition from the Collection of Paul Mellon*. New York, 1968.
Nixon List	The census of Caxton bindings published by Howard M. Nixon, "William Caxton and Bookbinding," in *Journal of the Printing Historical Society*, no. 11 (1976/77), pp. 92–113.

Oates	*A Catalogue of the Fifteenth-century Printed Books in the University Library Cambridge,* by J. C. T. Oates. Cambridge, 1954.
PML Ch L	*Check List of Fifteenth Century Printing in the Pierpont Morgan Library,* by Ada Thurston and Curt F. Bühler. New York, 1939.
Polain	*Catalogue des livres imprimés au quinzième siècle des bibliothèques de Belgique,* by Louis Polain. 4 vols. Brussels, 1932. And *Supplément.* Brussels, 1978.
Rhodes	*A Catalogue of Incunabula in All the Libraries of Oxford outside the Bodleian,* by Dennis E. Rhodes. Oxford, 1982.
Rosenwald	*The Lessing J. Rosenwald Collection: A Catalog of the Gifts of Lessing J. Rosenwald to the Library of Congress, 1943 to 1975.* Washington, 1977.
STC/STC²	*A Short-title Catalogue of Books Printed in England, Scotland, & Ireland . . . 1475–1640,* ed. A. W. Pollard and G. R. Redgrave. London, 1926. And *Second Edition, Revised & Enlarged,* ed. W. A. Jackson, F. S. Ferguson, and Katharine F. Pantzer, vol. 2. London, 1976.
Tract Vol.	Material itemized in Appendix B.
V–F	Jeanne Veyrin-Forrer, "Le deuxième atelier typographique de Paris: Cesaris et Stol," in *Gutenberg Jahrbuch* 1976:117–29.
VK	*Der Buchdruck Kölns bis zum Ende des fünfzehnten Jahrhunderts,* by Ernst Voulliéme. Bonn, 1903.

Notes

WILLIAM CAXTON, ENGLAND'S FIRST PRINTER

The best general study of Caxton is George D. Painter, *William Caxton, a Quincentenary Biography* (London, 1976), with extensive references to earlier literature. A concise and well-written introduction to the history of Caxton studies, and to modern methods and techniques for studying his printing, is Lotte Hellinga, *Caxton in Focus: The Beginning of Printing in England* (London, 1982), also with extensive references.

THE ROSENWALD SAMMELBAND AND OTHER CAXTON TRACT VOLUMES

The last two lots in Sotheby's sale of 20–21 May 1909 were 492, Beaumont and Fletcher's *Comedies and Tragedies*, London, 1647, F°, and 493, the Rosenwald Sammelband. A head-note identified them as "the Property of a Gentleman living in an old Manor House in the North . . . discovered in his library by the well-known booksellers Messrs. Jones & Evans, Queen Street, E.C." The description noted that "Some of the inner margins have been guarded with slips of old Latin books." Both lots were knocked down to one "E. Stanley," a name I do not recognize as belonging to the English book trade. It is possible that this was a nom de vente, disguising either a private buyer or bought-in lots that failed to reach their reserves.

A provisional list of identifiable Sammelbände containing Caxton's printing is given in Appendix A.

Additional brief information on the American owners of the Rosenwald Sammelband is given by Edwin Wolf and John F. Fleming, *Rosenbach: A Biography* (Cleveland and New York, 1960), 170, 180–81, 544. Concerning Mr. Rosenwald's gift to the Library of Congress, see *The Lessing J. Rosenwald Collection* (Washington, 1977), preface by Frederick R. Goff; and *Library of Congress Acquisitions: Rare Book and Special Collections Division, 1980* (Washington, 1982), by William Matheson.

AN UNRECORDED CAXTON INDULGENCE PRESERVED AS BINDER'S WASTE

Concerning the second colophon in the Rylands copy of *Dicts of the Philosophers*, dated 18 November 1477, see Lotte Hellinga, *Caxton in Focus*, 77–80. She demonstrates that this colophon was added later to the Rylands copy, in a printing operation separate from that of the remainder of the edition.

EARLY INDULGENCE PRINTING AND ITS SURVIVAL

The Mainz indulgences of 1454–55 are discussed, with a useful resumé of the extensive earlier literature, by Janet Ing, "The Mainz Indulgences of 1454/5: A Review of Recent Scholarship," *British Library Journal* 9 (1983): 14–31. Gottfried Zedler, *Die Mainzer Ablassbriefe der Jahre 1454 und 1455* (Mainz, 1913), includes a list of all then-known copies, manuscript or printed, of the Mainz indulgences, with notes on their purchasers and the amounts they contributed to acquire their indulgences, insofar as these are recorded.

The most comprehensive listing of fifteenth-century printed indulgence instruments is given by *Einblattdrucke des XV. Jahrhunderts* (Halle a.S., 1914); see index s.v. *Ablass, Ablassbriefe*. But many more examples have been discovered and recorded since 1914. Wolfgang Schmitz, *Die Kölner Einblattdrucke des XV. Jahrhunderts* (Cologne, 1979), includes a useful general survey of early indulgence printing, with references.

A lengthy (though incomplete) list of surviving copies of the folio St. Ambrose *Opera* (Basel: Joh. Amerbach, 1492) is given by GW 1599. The following fifteenth-century French editions of *Paris et Vienne* are known:

1. [Lyons: Guillaume Le Roy, ca. 1480]. F°. Claudin III, 43. *copy*: Agen, Bibliothèque Municipale.
2. [Lyons: Mathias Huss, ca. 1486]. 4°. Undescribed. *copy*: Pierpont Morgan Library (ex-Edmée Maus).
3. Antwerp: Gerard Leeu, 15 May 1487. F°. CA 941. *copies*: Paris, Bibliothèque Nationale; Vienna, Oesterreichische National-Bibliothek.
4. Paris: Denis Mellier [?before 1491]. 4°. Undescribed. *copy*: Otto Schäfer, Schweinfurt (ex-H. P. Kraus cat. 135, no. 6: in a Sammelband of ten French vernacular incunables, eight of which are unique and previously unrecorded). See *Katalog der Bibliothek Otto Schäfer*, ed. Manfred von Arnim, part 1 (Stuttgart, 1984), no. 262.
5. Paris: Denis Mellier, [ca. 1492–94]. 4°. Claudin II, 110. *copy*: Chantilly, Musée Condé (Delisle 1407).
6. Paris: Jean Trepperel [ca. 1498]. 4°. Goff P-113. *copy*: Pierpont Morgan Library.

Early editions in English, Dutch, and Italian of *Paris et Vienne* are of comparable rarity. The four fifteenth-century Dutch editions survive in a total of five copies; the three fifteenth-century Italian editions survive in one copy each. Caxton's English translation of the romance, printed by him in 1485 (Duff 337, Cx 82), survives in a single copy, as does Leeu's Antwerp reprint of 1492 (Duff 338, CA [II] 944a).

The Montserrat indulgences are discussed in detail by J. Rubio, "Butlles incunables de Montserrat," in *Analecta Montserratensia* 4 (1921): 263–77, and see also G. D. Painter's introduction to BMC X, pp. xvi, xliii, lxxiii. Documents relating to the Messina-printed Cefalù indulgences were printed by G. di Marzo, "Di Olivino e Lorenzo di Bruges, stampatori in Sicilia," in *Archivio storico Siciliano*, new ser., 4 (1879): 337–42. See also Victor Scholderer in the introduction to BMC VII, p. lxxiii, and Konrad Haebler, *Die Deutschen Buchdrucker des XV. Jahrhunderts im Auslande* (Munich, 1924), 151–52.

INDULGENCE PRINTING IN ENGLAND

Indulgences printed in England are listed in STC², s.v. *Indulgences*, but a number of additional unrecorded examples, including the Rounceval indulgence, have come to light since volume 2 of STC² appeared. Caxton's 1476 indulgence was published by A. W. Pollard, "The New Caxton Indulgence," in *The Library*, 4th ser., 9 (1928–29): 86–89. Long before this discovery was made, Pollard had suggested, presciently, that unrecorded printing by Caxton might well be found in the Public Record Office: see ibid., 3d ser., 1 (1910): 220. See also Kenneth Povey, "The Caxton Indulgence of 1476," ibid., 4th ser., 19 (1938–39): 462–64, which collates Caxton's text with that of two MS copies of the same indulgence, preserved as binder's waste in the Queen's University, Belfast. Other MS copies of this indulgence are in the Public Record Office, the archives of Westminster Abbey, and elsewhere. It may be noted that the purchasers of the single surviving copy of Caxton's edition of the indulgence, Henry and Katherine Langley, also acquired at least seven other indulgences (including two acquired by Katherine in her widowhood).

Detailed information on papal grants of indulgences for sale in England, their terms of validity, moneys raised from them, etc., is given by William E. Lunt, *Financial Relations of the Papacy with England, 1327–1534* (Cambridge, Mass., 1962), 447–620.

The 1480 Rhodes indulgences issued in England by John Kendale (Duff 204–8, STC² Ind. 107–11) present a text identical, mutatis mutandis, to many of the Rhodes indulgences printed and distributed on the Continent in 1480 and 1481, e.g., to those printed in Augsburg (*Einbl.* 1500–1501), Basel (*Einbl.* 1031), Cologne (*Einbl.* 776), Mainz (*Einbl.*

778), Memmingen (*Einbl.* 1502–1503), and Reutlingen (*Einbl.* 780).

THE HOSPITAL OF ST. MARY ROUNCEVAL

See generally Rotha M. Clay, *The Mediaeval Hospitals of England* (London, 1909), and the list of hospitals in David Knowles and R. Neville Hadcock, *Medieval Religious Houses: England and Wales* (London, 1953), 250–324. For the history of St. Mary Rounceval see in particular Herbert F. Westlake, *The Parish Gilds of Mediaeval England* (London, 1919), 92–103; Sir James Galloway, "The Hospital and Chapel of Saint Mary Roncevall at Charing Cross," in Royal Society of Medicine, *Proceedings* 6 (1912–13), Section of the History of Medicine, pp. 191–232; and London County Council, *Survey of London*, ed. Sir George Gater and Walter H. Godfrey, vol. 18 (London, 1937), 1–9. Westlake's *St. Margaret's Westminster: The Church of the House of Commons* (London, 1914) also contains information about St. Mary Rounceval.

The best general work on guilds is Westlake's *Parish Gilds*, cited immediately above. See also J. Toulmin Smith, ed., *English Gilds*, Early English Text Society, vol. 40 (London, 1870), particularly the introduction by Lujo Brentano.

Information on Edward Poynings is found in A. B. Emden, *Biographical Register of the University of Oxford to A.D. 1500*, 3 vols. (Oxford, 1957–59), s.v. There is a brief entry on John Kendale in the *Dictionary of National Biography*. John Lynton is a more obscure figure, but he may be identical with the man of that name, in the diocese of London, who in 1472 or 1473 was granted a "dispensatio ad incompatibilia" by Sixtus IV, i.e., was permitted by papal dispensation to hold canonically incompatible benefices (see *Calendar of Entries in the Papal Registers*, vol. 13 [1471–84], ed. J. A. Twemlow [London, 1955], p. 873).

INDULGENCES ISSUED BY ST. MARY ROUNCEVAL

On Chaucer's Rounceval Pardoner see J. J. Jusserand, *English Wayfaring Life in the Middle Ages* (London, 1889), 309–38, "The Pardoners," and J. M. Manly, *Some New Light on Chaucer* (London, 1926), 122 ff., "The Pardoner." The *Middle English Dictionary* (Ann Arbor, 1954–) provides, s.v. *pardoner*, an anthology of references, both literary and documentary. Alfred L. Kellogg and L. A. Haselmayer, "Chaucer's Satire of the Pardoner," in Modern Language Association, *Publications* 66 (1951): 251–77, is an excellent, detailed study of how pardoners in England practiced their trade, and of how their activities stood in relation to canon law.

For a grounding in the concept of confraternity, as it developed in monasteries, see Edmund Bishop, *Liturgica historica* (Oxford, 1918), 349–61, "Some Ancient Benedictine Confraternity Books." The standard study of English letters of fraternity is by J. C. Clark-Maxwell, "Some Letters of Confraternity," in *Archaeologia* 75 (1926): 19–60, and "Some Further Letters of Fraternity," ibid., 79 (1929): 179–216. Many printed letters of fraternity unknown to Clark-Maxwell are listed in STC², vol. 2, s.v. *Indulgences*. Three valuable studies of how the printing press was used to multiply letters of fraternity in the early sixteenth century are: William A. Jackson, "Three Printed English Indulgences at Harvard," in *Harvard Library Bulletin* 7 (1953): 229–31; D. M. Rogers, "The 'Friends of North Newington': A New Pynson Broadside," in *Bodleian Library Record* 5 (1954–56): 251–55; and D. E. Rhodes, "Some Documents Printed by Pynson for St. Botolph's, Boston, Lincs.," in *The Library*, 5th ser., 15 (1960): 53–57.

THE ROSENWALD SAMMELBAND REVISITED

A brief account of John Reynes is given by E. Gordon Duff, *The Printers, Stationers and Bookbinders of Westminster and London from 1476 to 1535* (Cambridge, 1906), 199–202, 232–34. More detailed studies of his bindings are: G. D. Hobson, *Blind-Stamped Panels in the English Book-Trade c. 1485–1555* (London: The Bibliographical Society, 1944), 31–39; J. Basil Oldham, *Shrewsbury School Library Bindings* (Oxford, 1943), 24 ff. (the Reynes binding which Oldham illustrates on pl. ix, Shrewsbury A.VII.20 covering a 1535 folio imprint, is virtually a twin of the Rosenwald binding); Oldham, *English Blind-Stamped Bindings* (Cambridge, 1952), see index s.v.; Oldham, *Blind Panels of English Binders* (Cambridge, 1958), see index s.v. The roll and three sizes of pineapple stamp used on the Rosenwald volume are most clearly illustrated by Oldham, *Shrewsbury*, pl. xlviii, nos. 58, 66–68; see also Oldham, *English Blind-Stamped Bindings*, pl. xxxvii, no. 553, and pl. lvii, no. 959.

The literature on Caxton's binder, or Caxton's bindery, as it might better be called, is extensive; by far the best single study is that of H. M. Nixon, "Caxton and Bookbinding," in Printing Historical Society, *Journal* 11 (1976): 92–113. At least one more binding from this shop has been identified since Nixon's article: the Sion College copy of Christine de Pisan, *Fayts of Arms*, Caxton, 14 July 1489, F° (Duff 96, Cx 90, DeR(C) 28.16), sold by Sotheby's, 13 June 1977, lot 14, illus.

For examples of Caxton's printing preserved only through the medium of binder's waste, see Appendix C.

ACKNOWLEDGMENTS I am grateful to Dr. Lotte Hellinga for bringing to my attention the Sotheby sale at which the Rosenwald Sammelband first appeared on the market, and for answering many questions relating to the list of Caxton tract volumes, Appendix B. Miss Katharine F. Pantzer and Dr. David Rogers shared their knowledge and records of later English printed indulgences. Mr. James E. Walsh examined for me the Houghton Library's copy of the 1530 Basel Pliny, to confirm the identity of the waste leaves in the Rosenwald volume. Mrs. Enid Nixon, with great kindness, searched out and sent photocopies of the Rounceval accounts preserved in the archives of Westminster Abbey. I have been given useful information also by Mme Jeanne Veyrin-Forrer, Dr. Christopher de Hamel, Dr. Jerome Machiels, Dr. Eva Irblich, and Mr. David J. McKitterick. The staff of the Library of Congress and of the Center for the Book have been unfailingly generous in their assistance: my particular thanks go to Mr. Thomas Albro, Dr. John Y. Cole, Mrs. Kathleen Mang, Mr. William Matheson, Ms. Evelyn Sinclair, and Mr. Peter Van Wingen.

Appendix A

The Text of the St. Mary Rounceval Indulgence

THE ROSENWALD SAMMELBAND is a volume of forty-nine quires: quires 1–13 = *Mirror of the World*; quires 14–23 = *Dicts of the Philosophers*; quires 24–39 = *Cicero*; quires 40–49 = *Cordiale*. Vellum quire guards, the cut-up strips of several copies of the Rounceval indulgence, survive in thirteen of these quires. (One of the strips contains no printing, and must have been cut from a blank margin of one of the indulgences.) Staining and traces of offset printer's ink are visible in the folds of every quire, showing that originally all of them had been similarly guarded with vellum strips; thus, only slightly more than a quarter of the original guards survive. The remainder were probably lost in the 1530s, when the original binding from Caxton's bindery was replaced in John Reynes's shop.

In the 1960s, Mr. Rosenwald had his Caxton volume sent to the Lakeside Bindery in Chicago for repairs, which involved disbinding and resewing. As part of these procedures, the quire guards were removed. A penciled note was written on each strip, except for the blank one, indicating its position in the volume at the time of disbinding. When the volume was reassembled the strips were sewn back into the quire folds, but no great care was taken to put the guards back in their original locations. Four of the twelve printed guards, namely those of quires 2, 4, 5, and 6, did return to their correct positions. The remainder were incorrectly repositioned, apparently at random. The special interest of the slips as printer's waste went unnoticed.

It is best, I think, to tag each indulgence strip according to the quire which it originally occupied. The blank strip is left out of the reckoning. It was resewn by the Lakeside Bindery into quire 49, where it certainly did not belong, but where it did belong can no longer be determined. The lines of the Rounceval indulgence attested by each slip are as follows (numbers in brackets indicate lines which, because of uneven cutting of the strips, are only partially represented):

SAMMELBAND QUIRE	=	INDULGENCE LINES
1	=	[1] 2–4 [5]
2	=	[1] 2–4 [5]
4	=	[5] 6–8 [9]
5	=	[11–12] 13–15 [16–17]
6	=	[9] 10–12 [13–14]
8	=	[1]
10	=	[18] 19–22 [23]
11	=	[8] 9–11 [12]
18	=	[1–2]
40	=	[6–8] 9–10 [11–12]
41	=	[6] 7–9 [10]
49	=	[1]

In three instances, two or more strips fit together precisely, showing that originally they were part of the same copies:

COPY 1		COPY 2		COPY 3	
quire 49		quire 8		quire 40	
quire 2		quire 1	lines 1–4	quire 5	lines 7–16
quire 4	lines 1–13				
quire 6					

Although their texts do not overlap, copies 2 and 3 must be distinct, for the gap between them, lines 5–6, is too narrow to have made up an intervening strip. This sort of calculation can, indeed, be carried still further. The strip of quire 41 contains lines 6–9, and therefore could not have belonged to copies 1 or 3; nor is it likely, for the reason given immediately above, to have belonged to copy 2: the gap between its line 6 and copy 2's line 4 is too wide to have been lost in cutting, but too narrow to have made up a now-missing strip. The vellum strip of quire 41 must therefore represent a fourth copy.

In fact, at least five copies of the Rounceval indulgence were probably originally contained within the Rosenwald volume. As indicated above, many of the quires—a dozen or more—though now lacking vellum guards, bear traces of printer's ink in their folds, indicating the original presence of printed waste. In four instances (and perhaps more, to a sharper eye than my own) the offsetting is sufficiently distinct, at some place or other, to be partly read in reverse:

SAMMELBAND QUIRE	=	INDULGENCE LINES
7	=	11–15
13	=	13
28	=	11–14
47	=	16–18

Three of these offsets, it will be noted, include line 13. These must all represent distinct copies, none of which can be identical to either of the existing copies 1 or 3. Here calculations must cease, having already, perhaps, become overly nice, but one other small point should be noticed. As the quire numbers of the strips constituting copies 1–3 show, when the indulgences were cut up in Caxton's bindery to make guards for this volume, a group of copies must have been all cut together and the resulting strips then taken up randomly for sewing.

Because four or more copies of the Rounceval indulgence supplied waste for the Rosenwald volume, some lines of the text are attested by more than one copy—for example, lines 7–9 are represented by the strips of quires 4, 40, and 41. None of these repetitions show any typographical variation.

Indulgences might be printed either for single or for plural use. That is, their phrasing might be adapted for sale either to a single individual or to more than one (most commonly, to a husband and wife). Caxton's Rounceval indulgence was designed for plural issue, as it contains such plural phrases as "deuocionis vestre" (rather than "tue"), line 7; and "vobis [not "tibi"] refundere cupientes," line 8. It was very common though not invariable practice to print indulgences in two distinct settings, one with wording for singular and one for plural use. Caxton may well, therefore, have printed a singular issue of the Rounceval indulgence, as well as the plural one that survives. His 1476 Jubilee indulgence (Cx 16) has a plural text and the unique surviving copy was in fact sold to a husband and wife, Henry and Katherine Langley. Caxton's first printing of the 1480 Rhodes indulgence (Cx 36) has a singular text, but the only known copy was nonetheless issued to a couple, Simon and Emma Mountfort. His second printing of the indulgence, with plural wording (Cx 43), was discovered as binder's waste at Trinity College, Cambridge, more than a century ago by Henry Bradshaw. Fragments of the corresponding singular issue (Cx 42) have turned up only in the last few years, again as binder's waste. (See Appendix C, nos. 2–3.)

The line-width of the Rounceval indulgence is 214 mm. A transcription of its text follows. Abbreviations have been expanded, as indicated by italics. Dots (. . .) indicate missing text. One typographical error has been corrected: in line 8, the compositor set a turned *n* in "refundere," producing "refuudere." At the beginning of each line is an indication, by quire number of the volume, of the strip or strips attesting that line.

ST. MARY ROUNCEVAL INDULGENCE

STRIP	LINE	
18; 49+2; 8+1	1	E⁴Dwardus ponyngis Cappellan*us* *do*mini regis/ Magister siue custos/ hospitalis b*eate* et gl*o*riose virg*inis* Marie
2; 1	2	de Rou*n*cideuall iuxta charingcrosse extra muros London*ii* situat*e*/ Ioha*n*nes Kendale valect*us* Corone dicti
2; 1	3	*do*mini regis/ et Ioha*n*nes Lynton *p*rocuratores generales ffrat*er*nitatis siue Gilde in honore dic*te* b*eate* et gloriose
2; 1	4	virginis Marie/ in Cappella siue hospitali predict*a* fu*n*dat*e* et stabilit*e*/ In *ch*rist*o* nob*is* Dilect*is* [29-mm space]
4	5	[61-mm space] Salut*em* et graci*am* *con*sequi semp*i*ternam/ Eloquio refere*n*te sacro/ didi-scim*us* qu*od* qua*n*ta bona
4; 41	6	spiritualia *per* dispe*n*satores ministerior*um* dei copiosi*us* distribuu*n*tur *ch*risticolis/ ta*n*to vberi*us* *per* opera pietatis graci*am* *con*ferunt
4; 41; 40	7	et i*n*ducunt/ Idcirco deuocionis *ves*tre feruorem quam ob dei reuere*n*ci*am* & gloriose virginis marie matris eius/ ad hospita =
4; 41; 40	8	le *nos*tr*um* habetis sinc*er*issime caritatis intuitu acceptantes/ Necno*n* et salutar*em* vic*em*/ vobis refundere cupientes/ Omniu*m*
4; 41; 40	9	bonor*um* spiritualiu*m*/ que *per* confratres et sorores nostras nu*n*c vel amodo dignabitur operari Cleme*n*cia saluatoris/ tam
6; 40	10	*in* vita qua*m* post mort*em* vos participes facim*us* *per* presentes/ videlicet o*m*nium missar*um*/ oraci*on*um/ Ieiunior*um*/ vigiliar*um*/ peregrina =

62

6	11	cionum*que* terre sancte *ch*risti sanguine *con*secrate / ac vrbis Romane sanctor*um* apostol*orum* et martirum sanguine rubricate /
5; 6	12	Vnde Clemens papa sextus de sua gracia speciali *con*cessit omnib*us* vere *con*fessis et *con*tritis de peccatis suis qui dicto hospi=
5; 6	13	tali / M*a*gistro et fratrib*us* eiusdem / toci*ens* quoci*ens* aliquid de bonis suis erogauerint / caritatiue seu assignauerint quouis=
5	14	modo / Aut se ascripserint *con*fraternitati eorum / Terci*am* part*em* de iniu*n*cta eis penitencia / tres a*n*nos et centu*m* dies indul=
5	15	gencie / Ceteru*m* alij qu*am* plures Romani pontifices / benefactorib*us* hospitalis predicte vna cu*m* dicto papa Clemente mise=
5	16	ricorditer *con*cesserunt plenam participacionem om*n*ium suffragior*um* spiritualiu*m* q*ue* fueru*n*t & de cetero fie*n*t in vniu*er*sali ecclesia / & Mille
5	17	. . . . & *per* sanctissi=
—	18(+?)	[missing]
10	19	p*ro* libito dispensare / ac *in* leuiora misericordit*er* com*m*utare / Iherosolimitane / petri et pauli / religionis & castitatis du*m*taxat
10	20	exceptis / Adicie*n*tes de gracia speciali / vt cu*m* obit*us* vestri cu*m* presentacione presenciu*m* in cappella siue hospitali predicta
10	21	fueri*n*t nu*n*ciati / Idem pro vobis fiet q*uo*d pro fratrib*us* et sororib*us* / Amicis & benefac- torib*us* n*o*stris defu*n*ctis ibidem com*m*uniter fac=
10	22	eri co*n*sueuit / In cuius rei testimoniu*m* Sigillu*m* procurator*um* generaliu*m* antedictor*um* / presentib*us* est appe*n*sum / Datu*m* in hospitali
10	23	. . . . Anno v*er*o M.CCCC. . . . .
—	24	[missing]

FIG. 18   The St. Mary Rounceval indulgence.

Appendix B

Caxton Tract Volumes—A Sample List

THE FOLLOWING LIST enumerates a group of tract volumes, both extant and dispersed, which contain or formerly contained one or more of Caxton's editions. The list is certainly not complete, having been compiled for the most part from secondary sources, and particularly from Seymour De Ricci's *Census of Caxtons*. The *Census* is a treasure trove of valuable information on the early provenances of copies, but it was impossible for De Ricci to see and closely examine every copy he recorded, so his work inevitably has errors and omissions.

The purpose in compiling such a sample list is experimental: I believe that early tract volumes, insofar as they survive, must be preserved, and considered, as unities, rather than as random collections of separable imprints; and where they do not survive, the labor of reconstructing them mentally, to the limits of the available evidence, is a valuable one. Virtually all catalogs of early printing take the single edition, not the volume, as their elemental. This is true whether they record the holdings of a single library (e.g., BMC) or of a country (Goff); whether they list the output of a press (Blades) or a group of presses in a city or region (VK, CA, Duff). For most bibliographical purposes, such edition-by-edition listing is eminently sensible, for editions are, so to speak, the fundamental units of book production. But when we move from the printing shop to the trade counter, and thence to the libraries of book buyers, other considerations come into play: it is the volume, not the edition, that constitutes the unit of ownership. When one finds a volume containing two or more separable editions, it is always useful to pose the questions: Why are they together? How early in the marketing process did they get that way?

Broadly considered (for in practice the variations of circumstance are many), multiple editions came into the covers of single bindings at either of two times: in the bookshop, when a purchase was first made; or later in the library, when an owner gathered together a group of unbound books or pamphlets and had a binding put on them, making thereby a conscious decision to further their preservation. Books in this latter category might have been purchased at many different times and places. The fact that they are in a Sammelband may not, therefore, directly reflect their marketing, though their common ownership may of itself be a matter of great interest. Books in the former category are even more closely interconnected: though their selection is ultimately due to the interests of the buyer, these are books that were available to that buyer at a single time, in a single shop.

The list below contains representatives of both categories. Such a volume as the Rosenwald Sammelband itself (no. 8 below) was certainly originally acquired in Caxton's shop, as Bishop Moore's volume of verse quartos (no. 3) must have been. The York Minster volume (no. 1) presents a more difficult but very interesting problem. Only two of its nine editions are Caxton's, and in English. The remaining seven editions are continental productions from three cities, Paris, Louvain, and Cologne; they are in Latin, and diverse in contents. But all are very close in date to the two Caxton tracts of 1476. It is likely that we have a clue here to the stock of an English bookseller, whether Caxton or another, around the year 1476.

By contrast, the volume of four Caxton editions and one Wynkyn de Worde edition (no. 37) is an owner's assemblage. That owner, R. Johnson, bought the books in 1510, long after they were printed, and the books themselves are not chronologically unified, dating variously between 1481 and ca. 1492. Johnson put a separate note of price in each book, suggesting that he had bought them individually. Here then, perhaps, we have a picture of what was available secondhand, almost twenty years after Caxton's death. Other volumes (see nos. 28, 29, 33) imply that certain of Caxton's late editions remained in print for several years after his death, just as we know that a service book whose printing he had commissioned in Paris, 1487, for English sale was still in stock after his death. Together, a group of volumes (nos. 19, 20, 21, 23, 34) show that many copies of Caxton's editions of *The Royal Book*, ca. 1485–86, and of *The Book of Good Manners*, 11 May 1487, were not sold until 1489 or after, reflecting from the standpoint of book marketing a still-mysterious and hitherto unrecognized slowdown in Caxton's printing and publishing activities during the years 1486–88.

Two pairs of Caxton-printed texts, very frequently found together, are omitted from the list, for their interrelations are such as to require a lengthier analysis: (1) the combination of *Chronicles of England* (Cx 39, 53) and *Description of Britain* (Cx 40); (2) the combination of John Mirk's *Festial* (Cx 65, 103) and the so-called *Quattuor Sermones* (Cx 54, 85, 104). The frequency with which these respective pairs of texts survive in common bindings indicates that, more often than not, they were marketed as single entities. In both instances, Caxton's marketing practices came to influence the practice of later publishers of the texts.

Chronicles of England and *Description of Britain*

Caxton's first edition of the *Chronicles of England* (Cx 39) was completed on 10 June 1480. Ten weeks later, on 18 August 1480, Caxton completed the brief *Description of Britain* (Cx 40), a text extracted from Ranulph Higden's *Polycronicon*, which he was to publish in full in 1482. Most surviving copies of the 1480 *Chronicles of England* are bound with the *Description of Britain*, and vice versa. Caxton must have presented the *Description* to his customers as a useful and inexpensive pendant to the substantial *Chronicles*. Two years later, on 8 October 1482, Caxton completed a second edition of the *Chronicles* (Cx 53), but he did not bother then to reprint the *Description of Britain*. A few copies of the 1482 *Chronicles* are bound with leftover copies of the *Description of Britain*, but most appear to have been sold alone. In the next years three more printers—William de Machlinia in London, ca. 1484 (Duff 99), the St. Albans Schoolmaster, ca. 1486 (Duff 101), and Gerard Leeu in Antwerp, 1493 (Duff 100)—issued editions of the *Chronicles of England*, all singly, without the *Description of Britain*.

Then in 1497–98 Caxton's successor, Wynkyn de Worde, reprinted both the *Chronicles* (Duff 102: 1497) and the *Description of Britain* (Duff 114: 1498). Although the two editions have separate quiring, and different dates, Wynkyn obviously looked on them as a natural pair, for the register of his *Chronicles* refers also to the *Description*; and most copies of the two editions survive bound together. All subsequent editions of the *Chronicles of England* were likewise in two parts, the first being the *Chronicles* proper, the second the *Description of Britain*. It should, however, be noted that the text of the *Chronicles* in Wynkyn's 1497 edition, and in all subsequent editions, was not Caxton's 1480–82 text but an independent compilation first printed by the St. Albans press.

John Mirk *Festial* and *Quattuor Sermones*

Mirk's *Festial* and the *Quattuor Sermones* present a more complex problem. The *Festial* is a collection of English homilies compiled in the early fifteenth century by John Mirk, prior of the Augustinian convent of Lilleshall, Shropshire. The homilies are assigned to the various feast days and Sundays of the year, and so compose a handy manual of sermon material for curates. Mirk's *Festial* continued to be a popular handbook for priests throughout the fifteenth century; it survives in numerous manuscript copies. The *Quattuor Sermones* is a less coherent text, and very inaptly named. Caxton's editions refer to it neither as "Quattuor Sermones" nor by any other title. The tag "Quattuor Sermones" was first applied to the text in the headlines of Wynkyn de Worde's reprint of 1493 (Duff 308). The title is inappropriate for several reasons: the text is not arranged in four sermons, nor is it either in Latin or based on a Latin source. The main part of *Quattuor Sermones* is an expanded paraphrase of a mid-fourteenth century Yorkshire devotional compendium known as the *Lay Folks' Catechism* or *Sermon of Dan John Gaytryge*. The paraphrase presented by Caxton (for which no direct manuscript source has been identified) might perhaps most naturally, by virtue of its thematic structure, be called something like "The Seven Things to Know God By." The remainder of Caxton's *Quattuor Sermones* consists of an anonymous sermon on the three parts of penance; a Commination service, or explanation of the sentence of excommunication; and two Sunday bidding prayers. It is plain that the *Quattuor Sermones*, like *Festial*, was a useful manual for curates, and so it is not surprising to find that most copies of the two texts are bound together.

Not until 1970 was it discovered that Caxton's supposed first edition of *Quattuor Sermones* (Duff 299) was in reality two separate editions, the one a line-for-line reprint of the other (Cx 54, 85).* A study of the paper stocks of the two editions reveals that an interval of some five years lies between them. The first edition of *Quattuor Sermones* was probably completed in late 1482 or early 1483, concurrently with Caxton's second edition of the *Canterbury Tales* (Cx 55). The second edition of *Quattuor Sermones* was completed in 1487, concurrently with the *Book of Good Manners* (Cx 84), and with several quarto service books for specific feast days (Cx 86, 87). This complicates considerably

*C. A. Webb, "Caxton's Quattuor Sermones: A Newly Discovered Edition," in *Essays in Honour of Victor Scholderer* (Mainz, 1970), 407–25. The same discovery was announced four years later, apparently in ignorance of Webb's publication, by Norman F. Blake and L. Reffkin, "Caxton's First Edition of Quattuor Sermones," in *Gutenberg Jahrbuch* 1974: 77–82. See also Norman F. Blake, ed., *Quattuor Sermones Printed by Caxton*, Middle English Texts 2 (Heidelberg, 1975), with useful information on the nature of the text. M. F. Wakelin, "The Manuscripts of Mirk's Festial," in *Leeds Studies in English*, new ser., 1 (1967), gives a detailed census of manuscript copies of *Festial*; none of these include Caxton's *Quattuor Sermones* text.

the question of the publishing relation between the *Festial* and the *Quattuor Sermones*. The first edition of the *Festial* was completed on 30 June 1483, that is, about six months after the first edition of *Quattuor Sermones* appeared. It survives in five copies, of which two are bound with the first edition of *Quattuor Sermones*, and three with the second edition. Two other copies of the first edition of *Quattuor Sermones* were not bound with the *Festial* (cf. nos. 12 and 13 below).

This combination of circumstances suggests the following sequence of printing and publishing: (a) *Quattuor Sermones* began to be sold as soon as it was ready, in late 1482 or early 1483. (b) After *Festial* was completed, some six months later, Caxton publicized it as forming a natural entity with his already existing priest's manual, *Quattuor Sermones*. Many customers bought the two texts together. (c) By 1487, the first edition of *Quattuor Sermones* was sold out, but there was still a substantial remnant of copies of *Festial* in stock, for the better sale of which a second edition of *Quattuor Sermones* was produced.

In 1491, shortly before his death, Caxton produced a second edition of Mirk's *Festial* (Cx 103) and a third edition of *Quattuor Sermones* (Cx 104). These clearly were intended to be sold together. Of the six surviving copies of *Festial*[2], four are bound with *Quattuor Sermones*[3], one is bound with a leftover copy of the 1487 *Quattuor Sermones*[2], and one is alone. Caxton's 1491 *Festial* was not, by the way, a reprint of his 1483 edition. It is based rather on a 1486 edition by the Oxford printer Theodoric Rood (Duff 300), which represents a distinctly different recension, and which Caxton further modified. After Caxton's death many more editions of *Festial* were published by various printers and booksellers into the 1530s, and these invariably were accompanied by the *Quattuor Sermones*, either within the same edition or as a subsidiary edition.

In both cases, therefore—*Chronicles of England* and *Description of Britain*, *Festial* and *Quattuor Sermones*—the marketing and publishing practices of Caxton gradually created, from what had been singular and independent texts, unified combinations which eventually were looked on, by publishers and book buyers, as standard entities. In the case of *Chronicles-Description*, the combination owes more to Wynkyn de Worde than to Caxton himself, although Caxton set the precedent for combining the two. The chief evidence for these processes lies in the surviving tract volumes joining the texts. To the extent that the original tract volumes have been broken up by later negligence and ignorance, the steps in the process become correspondingly more difficult to discover and retrace.

The sample list that follows attempts to put a group of Caxton tract volumes before the reader's eyes. The format of each volume is given, and it is named by its earliest clearly identified owner. As will be seen, such nomenclature is often more or less notional, for original ownership can rarely be specified. Contents are listed by order of binding, where this information is available. The extent of each edition is given, by count of leaves. A quire count is also given, for this is the way the binder would have looked at the assemblage: so many quires to be sewn.

CAXTON TRACT VOLUMES

1. YORK MINSTER. 4°. Disbound, partly dispersed. The volume probably came to York Minster by the bequest of Tobie Matthew (1546–1628), archbishop of York. The contents were separately rebound, through T. F. Dibdin's agency, by Charles Lewis, 1816 (see Dibdin, *Bibliographical Decameron* 3: 817 ff.). The instructions to the binder survive, and from them Bernard Barr, sub-librarian of York Minster, has reconstructed the contents as follows (see J. Veyrin-Forrer, "Caxton and France," in Printing Historical Society, *Journal*, 1976/77, no. 11: 32, note 2; I have made several minor corrections to the reconstruction as published there). Nos. 1–7 are still at York Minster; nos. 8 and 9 were sold in 1930 to A. S. W. Rosenbach and are now in the Pierpont Morgan Library.

		LEAVES	QUIRES
1	ps.-Seneca. *De remediis fortunae.* [Paris: P. Caesaris & J. Stol, ca. 1474–75] Polain 3492, V-F 18.	10	1
2	Ant. Liporita. *Formula exordiorum.* [Paris: P. Caesaris, ca. 1476–77] Hain 10115, V-F 23.	36	4
3	Vergerius. *De ingenuis moribus.* [Louvain:] Joh. de Westfalia, [ca. 1476–77] Goff V-131, CA 1724.	44	6
4	Fr. Florius. *De amore Camilli et Aemiliae.* [Paris: P. Caesaris & J. Stol, ca. 1473] Goff F-229, V-F 1.	50	5
5	Pius II (Aeneas Sylvius). *De miseria curialium.* [Paris: P. Caesaris & J. Stol, ca. 1475] V-F 17a: unique.	30	3
6	Innocent IV. *Tractatus exceptionum.* [Paris: Au Soufflet Vert, ca. 1475–77] Undescribed and otherwise unrecorded.	10	1
7	Peter of Blois. *De amicitia Christianorum.* [Cologne: Pr. of Historia sancti Albani, ca. 1473–74] Goff P-455, VK 914.	16	2
8	J. Lydgate. *The Horse, the Sheep and the Goose*[1]. [W. Caxton, 1476] Cx 14, Duff 262, DeR 70.1, PML Ch L 1764.	18	2
9	J. Lydgate. *The Churl and the Bird*[1]. [W. Caxton, 1476] Cx 13, Duff 257, DeR 67.1, PML Ch L 1765.	10	1

2. HARLEY. 4°. ?Disbound. The Harleian Library was the joint formation of Robert Harley, earl of Oxford (1661–1724), and of his son Edward Harley, 2d earl (1689–1741), the latter of whom was an assiduous collector of Caxton's printing. The present volume was in the Harleys' time in "original vellum wrapper" (DeR), but may once have been bound with other quartos. The volume was later in the library of William Cavendish, 6th duke of Devonshire (1790–1858), and during his tenure was rebound by Charles Lewis. It is now in the Huntington Library.

		LEAVES	QUIRES
1	Cato. *Disticha*[1], Lat.-Eng. [1476] Cx 12, Duff 77, DeR 14.1, Mead 5218.	34	4
2	J. Lydgate. *Stans puer ad mensam*, Eng. [?1476] Cx 15, Duff 269, DeR 74.2, Mead 5219.	4	1

3. BISHOP MOORE. 4°. Disbound. The enormous library of John Moore (1646–1714), bishop of Ely, was purchased after his death by George I, and presented to Cambridge University. This volume was broken up in the nineteenth century. Miscellaneous early signatures in the volume include John Fawler (and MS verse in his hand), Arundell, Paul Haynes, Magister Birkhened, Thomas Bristow, Thomas Halm, Waterhouse, George Ferrers.

		LEAVES	QUIRES
1	J. Lydgate. *Stans puer ad mensam*, Eng. [?1476] Cx 15, Duff 269, DeR 74.1, Oates 4070.	4	1
2	Cato. *Disticha*[2], Lat.-Eng. [1477] Cx 22, Duff 76, DeR 13.1, Oates 4066.	34	4
3	J. Lydgate. *The Churl and the Bird*[2]. [1477] Cx 19, Duff 256, DeR 66.1, Oates 4062.	10	1
4	J. Lydgate. *The Horse, the Sheep and the Goose*[2]. [1477] Cx 18, Duff 261, DeR 69.1, Oates 4061.	18	2
5	J. Lydgate. *The Temple of Glass*. [1477] Cx 21, Duff 270, DeR 75.1, Oates 4068.	34	4
6	G. Chaucer. *The Temple of Brass* (etc.) [1477] Cx 27, Duff 93, DeR 25.1, Oates 4063.	24+?	3+?
7	*The Book of Courtesy*. [1477] Cx 29, Duff 53, DeR 11.1, Oates 4065.	14	2
8	G. Chaucer. *Queen Anelida and the False Arcite* (etc.) [1477] Cx 28, Duff 92, DeR 24.1, Oates 4067.	10	1

4. HARLEY. 4°. Disbound, dispersed. In a Harleian binding. Early MS headlines identify it as "liber xiij" of a Sammelband. Later in the Göttingen University Library; sold in 1929 to the Pierpont Morgan Library.

		LEAVES	QUIRES
1	*Infancia salvatoris*. [1477] Cx 20, Duff 222, DeR 62.1, PML Ch L 1761.	18	2

2, etc. Unidentified.

5. HARLEY. F°. Disbound. Probably collected by Edward Harley, 2d earl of Oxford; then through various hands until acquired in late nineteenth century by Lord Amherst of Hackney. His Caxtons sold en bloc to Pierpont Morgan, immediately before the Sotheby's sale of Lord Amherst's library, 3 December 1908, the catalog of which included the preempted Caxton volumes. Shortly after the present volume arrived in Morgan's library, no. 2 was removed and bound separately.

		LEAVES	QUIRES
1	*Dicts and Sayings of the Philosophers*[1]. Before 18 November 1477. Cx 26, Duff 123, DeR 36.9, PML Ch L 1759a.	78	10
2	Christine de Pisan. *Moral Proverbs*. 20 February 1478. Cx 30, Duff 95, DeR 27.1, PML Ch L 1763.	4	1

6. WILLIAM EBESHAM. 4°. Disbound, dispersed. William Ebesham, fl. 1464–97, was a professional scribe, long resident in Westminster; two codices in his hand were bound by Caxton's bindery (see A. I. Doyle, "The Work of a Late 15th-century English Scribe, William Ebesham," in John Rylands Library, *Bulletin* 39 [1956–57]: 298–325, the present tract volume described pp. 308–12). No. 3 in this volume, the only surviving copy of its edition, was still intact and perhaps complete when the volume was offered for sale by Thomas Osborne in the 1750s and 1760s. By the time the volume was auctioned at John Brand's sale, 1807, no. 3 had been removed and was lost from sight until it was acquired by the British Museum in 1851. The remainder of the volume went from Brand to the Marquess of Blandford, then to Earl Spencer, then (see no. 14 below) to the John Rylands Library.

		LEAVES	QUIRES
1	Manuscript: religious miscellany, written by Ebesham, including works of Richard Rolle, etc. Rylands MS lat. 395.	?138	?11
2	John Russell. *Propositio*. [1476] Cx 10, Duff 367, DeR 90.1, Rylands 18932.	4	1
3	*Officium visitationis BMV*. [1480] Cx 37, Duff 148, DeR 43.1, BL IA. 55065 (only 7 leaves of the final, 8-leaf quire survive). NB: Both nos. 2 and 3 contain additional writing in Ebesham's hand.	?3	?24

7. RIPON CATHEDRAL. F°. Disbound, dispersed. Seen by T. F. Dibdin (*Bibliographical Decameron* 3, 420) in 1815, disbound and individually rebound, through his agency, by Charles Lewis. No. 1 is still at Ripon. No. 2 was sold by the Cathedral at Sotheby's, 31 May 1960, lot 5, and acquired by H. P. Kraus. He traded it to Cambridge University Library in exchange for one of their two copies of Caxton's Bruges-printed *Recuyell of the History of Troy* (Duff 242, DeR 3.5, Oates 3837), which was then sold to Paul Mellon and is now in the Yale Center for British Art (Mellon 1). Early owners' names in nos. 1 and 2 include John Whyt, Francis Howard, Ambrose Niclas, Nicholas Morgan.

		LEAVES	QUIRES
1	Boethius. *The Consolation of Philosophy*. [1478] Cx 31, Duff 47, DeR 8.13, Ripon Cathedral.	94	12
2	*The Doctrine to Learn French and English*. [1480] Cx 41, Duff 405, DeR 97.1, ULC.	26	3

8. ROSENWALD. F°. Intact. Mr. Rosenwald's gift to the Library of Congress (see pp. 20–21 above for earlier provenance). Bound by John Reynes, ca. 1535; formerly bound by Caxton's bindery. Contain's printer's waste and bookseller's waste (see also Appendix A, above).

		LEAVES	QUIRES
1	*The Mirror of the World*[1]. After 8 March [ca. October] 1481. Cx 46, Duff 401, Rosenwald 563.	100	13
2	*Dicts and Sayings of the Philosophers*[2]. "18 November 1477" [ca. June 1480] Cx 38, Duff 124, Rosenwald 560.	78	10
3	Cicero. *Of Old Age* (etc.) 12 August [–ca. September] 1481. Cx 45, Duff 103, Rosenwald 562.	120	16
4	*Cordiale of the Four Last Things.* 24 March 1479. Cx 34, Duff 109, Rosenwald 559.	78	10
5	Indulgence. Hospital of St. Mary Rounceval: letter of confraternity. [1480]. Fragmentary: printer's waste. Cx 44, Bdr's Waste 1.	—	—

9. HARDWICKE. F°. Disbound. Owned by Philip Yorke, 1st earl of Hardwicke (1690–1764), lord
    chancellor. Auctioned by Christie's, 29 June 1888, lot 116, acquired by Quaritch and broken up. The
location of no. 1 has not been determined. No. 2, seriously imperfect, was used with other leaves of separate
provenance to make up a partial volume of Cicero, now in the Pierpont Morgan Library.

		LEAVES	QUIRES
1	*Mirror of the World*[1]. After 8 March [ca. October] 1481. Cx 46, Duff 401, DeR 94.33.	100	13
2	Cicero. *Of Old Age* (etc.) 12 August [–ca. September] 1481. Cx 45, Duff 103, DeR 31.39=31.25 (part), PML Ch L 1772.	120	16

10. MAURICE JOHNSON. F°. Disbound and dispersed. Maurice Johnson (1688–1755) was an
     antiquary of Spalding, Lincs. This volume was broken up at the time it came on the market, 1898. The
sequence of copies given below is arbitrary. Nos. 1 and 2 were acquired by the British Museum, the remainder by the executors of W. H. Christie-Miller, for the Britwell Court library. The latter were auctioned at
the Christie-Miller sale of 16 December 1919. Nos. 3 and 4 were acquired at that time by J. P. Morgan, and
are now in the Pierpont Morgan Library. No. 5 was later in the collection of Sir Arthur Howard, and no. 6
later in the collection of Hannah D. Rabinowitz. They were acquired through separate channels by Paul
Mellon and are now in the Yale Center for British Art.

		LEAVES	QUIRES
1	Cato. *Disticha*[3], Lat.-Eng. [1483] Cx 56, Duff 78, DeR 15.1, BL IB. 55034.	28	4
2	J. Lydgate. *The Court of Sapience.* [1483] Cx 61, Duff 260, DeR 68.3, BL IB. 55055.	40	5
3	Alain Chartier. *Le Curial*, Eng. [1483] Cx 58, Duff 84, DeR 20.2, PML Ch L 1784.	6	1
4	*Reynard the Fox*[1]. After 6 June 1481 [1482] Cx 51, Duff 358, DeR 87.6, PML Ch L 1771.	85	11
5	Jac. de Cessolis. *The Game and Play of Chess*[2]. [1483] Cx 57, Duff 82, DeR 18.2, Mellon 8.	84	11
6	Cato. *Disticha*, tr. Caxton. After 23 December 1483 [1484] Cx 68, Duff 79, DeR 16.12, Mellon 10.	78	10

11. EXETER COLLEGE. F°. Intact. Shelf-mark 9M.4815. The first text bears on its title page the
early signature of Lodovicus Johannes.

		LEAVES	QUIRES
1	St. Catherine of Siena. *The Orchard of Syon.*	176	29
	Wynkyn de Worde, 28 September 1519.		
	STC 4815.		
2	Cato. *Disticha*, tr. Caxton. After 23 December 1483 [1484]	78	10
	Cx 68, Duff 79, DeR 16.7, Rhodes 527.		
3	Boethius. *The Consolation of Philosophy.* [1478]	94	12
	Cx 31, Duff 47, DeR 8.7, Rhodes 402(a).		
4	J. Lydgate. *The Life of Our Lady.* [1483]	96	13
	Cx 63, Duff 266, DeR 71.4, Rhodes 1131.		

12. ROGER THORNEY. F°. Intact. Roger Thorney (d. 1515) was a mercer of London and patron
of Wynkyn de Worde. No. 4 in this volume served as printer's copy for Wynkyn's edition of Lydgate's *Siege of Thebes*, ca. 1500, 4° (Duff 268): see G. Bone, "Extant Manuscripts Printed from by W. de
Worde with Notes on the Owner, Roger Thorney" in *The Library*, 4th ser., 12 (1931–32): 284–306. The
volume belonged later to William Myddelton, fl. 1530, who married Thorney's widow Eleanor, and then
to Sir William Paddy (d. 1634), who gave and bequeathed many books, including this one, to St. John's,
Oxford. Shelf-mark: b.2.21.

		LEAVES	QUIRES
1	G. Chaucer. *The Canterbury Tales* [2]. [1483]	312	40
	Cx 55, Duff 88, DeR 23.1, Rhodes 538.		
2	G. Chaucer. *Troilus and Criseyde.* [1483]	120	15
	Cx 60, Duff 94, DeR 26.1, Rhodes 539.		
3	*Quattuor sermones*[1], Eng. [1482–83]	30	4
	Cx 54, Duff 299[a], DeR 85.2, Rhodes 1202.		
4	[MS on paper, ?1475–80]. J. Lydgate. *Siege of Thebes.*	60+	?

13. VIENNA, OESTERREICHISCHE NATIONALBIBLIOTHEK. F°. Disbound. Of the
several Caxton editions in the Austrian National Library (ÖNB), the three listed below were apparently acquired, already separately bound, by a single purchase of the late eighteenth or early nineteenth
century. Their leaf dimensions are almost identical, and nos. 1 and 2 are identically bound. No. 3 bears on
its last leaf a formulaic inscription in an early hand in the name of "roberd ratlef af nonyeton" (i.e., Nuneaton,
Warwickshire). Nos. 1 and 2 are more likely than not to have originally belonged together, and no. 3 may
also have formed part of the same volume.

		LEAVES	QUIRES
1	*Quattuor sermones*[1], Eng. [1482–83]	30	4
	Cx 54, Duff 299[a], DeR 85.4, ÖNB Ink.2.D.28.		
2	G. Chaucer. *The Book of Fame.* [1483]	30	4
	Cx 59, Duff 86, DeR 21.3, ÖNB Ink.2.D.27.		
3	J. de Cessolis. *The Game and Play of Chess* [2]. [1483]	84	11
	Cx 57, Duff 82, DeR 18.10, ÖNB Ink.2.D.26.		

14. COCHRANE. F°. Disbound, dispersed. J. G. Cochrane, London bookseller. This volume was sold, 1813, to George John Spencer, 2d earl Spencer (1758–1834), greatest collector of—and greatest tamperer with—Caxton's printing. His books became (1892) one of the foundation collections of the John Rylands Library, now part of the University of Manchester. Lord Spencer had the contents of this volume individually rebound by Charles Lewis. He gave no. 3 from the volume to the duke of Devonshire, and it is now in the Huntington Library.

		LEAVES	QUIRES
1	Cato. *Disticha*[3], Lat.-Eng. [1483] Cx 56, Duff 78, DeR 15.3.	28	4
2	A. Chartier. *Le Curial*, Eng. [1483] Cx 58, Duff 84, DeR 20.3.	6	1
3	*The Doctrine to Learn French and English.* [1480] Cx 41, Duff 405, DeR 97.4, Mead 5234.	26	3

15. THOMAS RAWLINSON. F°. Disbound, dispersed. Thomas Rawlinson (1681–1725), book collector. The four copies below all apparently belonged to Rawlinson; whether they were then in a single volume or already broken up is uncertain. They are foliated in a single sequence by an early hand. Lacunae in the foliation show that before no. 1 there was originally a text of ca. 40 leaves; between nos. 2 and 3 a text of ca. 10 leaves; between nos. 3 and 4 a text of ca. 17 leaves. These missing texts have not been identified. After passing through various later hands, nos. 1–3 were all acquired by George III, whose library was given to the British Museum in 1826 by George IV; no. 4 was acquired by the Rev. C. M. Cracherode, whose library was bequeathed to the British Museum.

		LEAVES	QUIRES
1	G. Chaucer. *The Book of Fame.* [1483] Cx 59, Duff 86, DeR 21.1=.5=.6, BL IB. 55097.	30	4
2	A. Chartier. *Le Curial*, Eng. [1483] Cx 58, Duff 84, DeR 20.4, BL IB. 55100.	6	1
3	*The Life of St. Winifred.* [1484] Cx 73, Duff 414, DeR 100.2, BL IB. 55109.	16	2
4	*The Book of Eneydos.* After 22 June 1490. Cx 97, Duff 404, DeR 96.7, BL IB. 55135.	86	12

16. MOSES PITT. F°. Intact. Bodleian Library Arch. G. d. 13, the gift of Moses Pitt, London bookseller, 1680.

		LEAVES	QUIRES
1	Cato. *Disticha*, tr. Caxton. After 23 December 1483 [1484] Cx 68, Duff 79, DeR 16.30. 25 folios only.	78	10
2	Boethius. *The Consolation of Philosophy.* [1478] Cx 31, Duff 47, DeR 8.12.	94	12
3	*The Knight of the Tower.* 31 January 1484. Cx 69, Duff 241, DeR 63.6.	106	14
4	Aesop. *Fables.* 26 March 1484. Cx 70, Duff 4, DeR 4.3.	144	18

17. OLD ROYAL LIBRARY. 4°. Disbound. British Library, old shelf-mark C.21.c.2. The Old
    Royal Library consists of the collections of English monarchs from Edward IV onward (except as
otherwise dispersed) presented by George II to the British Museum in the 1750s as one of its foundation
collections. These two texts apparently were once bound with additional tracts, unidentified.

		LEAVES	QUIRES
1	*The Order of Chivalry*. [1484] Cx 71, Duff 58, DeR 81.1, BL IA. 55071.	52	7
2	*Revelation of St. Nicholas*. William de Machlinia, [1484] Duff 357, BL IA. 55449.	66	8
3,	etc. Unidentified.	?	?

18. DANSER. F°. Disbound. All that is known of Danser is that he sold this volume to John Bagford,
    18 July 1700. It was later perhaps in Bishop Moore's library, then in the Harleian library, where it
was broken up. The two texts were acquired separately by George III in the 1770s, and rebound at his
instance. Both are now in the British Library.

		LEAVES	QUIRES
1	*The History of Charles the Great*. 1 December 1485. Cx 81, Duff 83, DeR 19.1, BL C.10.b.9.	96	12
2	*Paris and Vienne*. 19 December 1485. Cx 82, Duff 337, DeR 83.1, BL C.10.b.10.	36	5

19. BISHOP MOORE. F°. Disbound. Nos. 1–3 at Cambridge University Library. No. 4 disposed of
    to Henry Huth, 1870, and now in the Pierpont Morgan Library.

		LEAVES	QUIRES
1	*The Royal Book*. [1485–86] Cx 83, Duff 366, DeR 89.2, Oates 4100.	162	20
2	Jacques Le Grand. *The Book of Good Manners*. 11 May 1487. Cx 84, Duff 248, DeR 65.1, Oates 4103.	66	8
3	*Dicts and Sayings of the Philosophers*[3]. [1489] Cx 93, Duff 125, DeR 39.5, Oates 4109.	70	10
4	*The Doctrinal of Sapience*. After 7 May 1489. Cx 94, Duff 127, DeR 40.7, PML ChL 1791a.	92	11

20. WHITLEY BEAUMONT. F°. Disbound and dispersed. Sold Hodgson's, 23 Nov. 1906, lot 188,
    to Quaritch for British Museum. Originally in a Cambridge binding (Unicorn Bindery), which
stayed with no. 2 in the British Museum. No. 1 may be the later Boies Penrose copy; no. 3 is at the University of Illinois.

		LEAVES	QUIRES
1	*The Royal Book*. [1485–86] Cx 83, Duff 366, DeR 89.10: lacking "61 leaves at the beginning." The Penrose copy (auctioned in Basel, 25 September 1978, lot 8, and again at Sotheby's, London, 27 June 1985, lot 36) lacks 75 leaves at beginning, viz., quires a–i + k 1–3, and also q 8.	162	20

		LEAVES	QUIRES
2	Jacques Le Grand. *The Book of Good Manners.* 11 May 1487. Cx 84, Duff 248, DeR 65.4, BL IB. 55125.	66	8
3	*The Doctrinal of Sapience.* After 7 May 1489. Cx 94, Duff 127, DeR 40.12. Lacks 39 leaves.	92	11

21. LAMBETH PALACE. Fº. Intact. NB: The volume contains one leaf from Cato, *Disticha*, tr. Caxton [1484], Cx 68, Duff 79, which may be binder's waste from the original binding.

		LEAVES	QUIRES
1	*Dicts and Sayings of the Philosophers*[3]. [1489] Cx 93, Duff 125, DeR 39.3.	70	10
2	Jacques Le Grand. *The Book of Good Manners.* 11 May 1487. Cx 84, Duff 248, DeR 65.3.	66	8

22. SOTHERAN. Fº. Disbound, dispersed. Henry Sotheran, London bookseller. Acquired by him from "a lady," 1868, according to De Ricci, and apparently dismantled by him. No. 1 was sold to Henry Huth, and is now in the Pierpont Morgan Library; no. 2 is unlocated, or unidentified.

		LEAVES	QUIRES
1	Jac. de Cessolis. *The Game and Play of Chess*[2]. [1483] Cx 57, Duff 82, DeR 18.12, PML Ch L 1775.	84	11
2	Christine de Pisan. *Fayts of Arms.* 14 July 1489. Cx 90, Duff 96, DeR 28.37.	144	19

23. JOHN RATCLIFFE. Fº. Disbound, dispersed. John Ratcliffe, chandler, of Bermondsey. His library was auctioned by James Christie, 27 March 1776, the present volume being lot 1661, bought by Gustavus Brander, and apparently disbound by him. In Brander's sale, Leigh & Sotheby, 8 February 1790, no. 1 was lot 1013; it is now in the John Carter Brown Library. No. 2 was lot 1012, and was bought by Francis Douce. In both the Ratcliffe and the Brander sales, the text of no. 2 was identified as "Politick Admonitions and Observations Fit for Great Men to Peruse," printed by Caxton, imperfect. De Ricci suggests with fair plausibility that this was *The Doctrinal of Sapience*, of which Douce possessed an imperfect copy, bequeathed to the Bodleian Library.

		LEAVES	QUIRES
1	*The Royal Book.* [1485–86] Cx 83, Duff 366, DeR 89.9. John Carter Brown Library.	162	20
2	?*The Doctrinal of Sapience.* After 7 May 1489. Cx 94, Duff 127, ?DeR 40.9 = Bodleian Douce 148.	92	11

24. JAMES WEST. Fº. Disbound. James West (1704–1773), of the Inner Temple, was president of the Royal Society and an omnivorous collector. This volume was acquired later by Earl Spencer and disbound at his instance; it is now in the Rylands Library.

		LEAVES	QUIRES
1	G. de Deguilleville. *The Pilgrimage of the Soul.* 6 June 1483. Cx 64, Duff 267, DeR 73.2.	114	15

2 *Deathbed Prayers.* [?1484]   1   —
   Cx 74, Duff 122, DeR 34.1. Bd. into no. 1, above.
3 *The Art and Craft of Dying.* After 15 June 1490.   14   3
   Cx 98, Duff 35, DeR 6.3.

25. JOHN SELDEN. F°. Intact. John Selden (1584–1654), polymath jurist, parliamentarian, orientalist. His collections were bequeathed to the Bodleian Library. Shelf-mark, S. Seld. d. 11.

	LEAVES	QUIRES
1 *The Art and Craft of Dying.* After 15 June 1490. Cx 98, Duff 35, DeR 6.4.	14	3
2 C. Maydeston. *Directorium sacerdotum.* [1489] Cx 91, Duff 292, DeR 78.1.	194	24

26. NATHANIEL CRYNES. F°. Intact. Nathaniel Crynes (1686–1745), fellow of St. John's, Oxford. Bequeathed to St. John's, shelf-mark b.2.24. No. 5 contains the signature of Thomas Tanner (1674–1735), bishop of St. Asaph, cf. no. 28 below.

	LEAVES	QUIRES
1 Cato. *Disticha*[3], Lat.-Eng. [1483] Cx 56, Duff 78, DeR 15.2, Rhodes 526.	28	4
2 J. Lydgate. *The Court of Sapience.* [1483] Cx 61, Duff 260, DeR 68.2, Rhodes 1130.	40	5
3 J. Lydgate. "A Calendar." MS on paper, late fifteenth century, incomplete.	5	[1]
4 Guillaume de Deguilleville. *The Pilgrimage of the Soul.* 6 June 1483. Cx 64, Duff 267, DeR 73.4, Rhodes 882.	114	15
5 *The Book of Eneydos.* After 22 June 1490. Cx 97, Duff 404, DeR 96.13, Rhodes 1832.	86	12

27. ANTHONY HIGGIN. F°. Disbound, dispersed. Bequeathed to Ripon Cathedral by Anthony Higgin (d. 1624), dean of the Collegiate Church; probably collected by him in his student days at St. John's, Cambridge. Rebound in the early nineteenth century, but left intact. Disbound and broken up at the bindery of the British Museum, 1952. No. 1 was given to the British Museum (now British Library); nos. 2, 3, and 5 seem to have returned to Ripon Cathedral. No. 4 was sold by Ripon Cathedral at Sotheby's, 31 May 1960, lot 6, and acquired by Quaritch for the Brotherton Library, University of Leeds. Besides these five codices, the Higgin Sammelband contained four short MS texts written on various blank pages within the volume: (*a*) copy of a letter of confraternity from John Auckland, prior of Durham, to John Portar, 1484; (*b*) an account of a case of demoniacal possession; (*c*) "A Lytyll Ballet Made of the Yong Dukes Grace" (viz., Henry Fitzroy, bastard son of Henry VIII, 1519–1536), set to music; (*d*) "A Ballet of the Deth of the Cardynall" (viz., Wolsey, ca. 1475–1530), set to music. Of these, items *a*, *c*, and *d* were printed in the *Yorkshire Archaeological Journal* 2: 395–97. Item *d* is written on the blank verso of fo. 34 (?recte, 35) of no. 4, and on a following blank leaf (?fol. 36 of no. 4), and thus is preserved at Leeds. The two tracts making up no. 3 in this volume were separated in the nineteenth-century rebinding, and the second of them was bound in at the end of the volume, but they were probably integral in the earlier

binding. See R. H. Martin and J. E. Mortimer, *The Epitome Margaritae Eloquentiae of Laurentius Gulielmus de Saona* (offprint of Leeds Philosophical and Literary Society, *Proceedings*, Literary and Historical Section, vol. 14, part 4 [1971], 99–187) and J. E. Mortimer, *The Library Catalogue of Anthony Higgin, Dean of Ripon (1608–1624)* (ibid., vol. 10, part 1 [1962], 1–75, at pp. 44–45).

		LEAVES	QUIRES
1	J. Gerson. *De consolatione theologiae.* Cologne: Joh. Koelhoff, 27 January 1488. Goff B-783, pt. II (pt. I= Boethius, *De consolatione philosophiae*). The two parts have separate quiring, and various other copies are known consisting of part I or part II only. British Library (Department of Manuscripts).		24	3
2	Ephrem Syrus. *De compunctione cordis,* etc. [Freiburg i. Br.: Kil. Piscator, not after 1491] Goff E-44.		20	3
3	[*Tractatus VI de confessione,* etc.] 2 parts only: 1. Ant. de Butrio. *Speculum de confessione*; 6. Dionysius Cartus. *Speculum conversionis peccatorum.* Louvain: Joh. de Westfalia, [ca. 1483–85]. Goff B-1387, CA 391 + 589. The six tracts of this volume have consecutively signed quiring, a-y, but various copies consist of only a selection of the tracts.		28 / 14	4 / 2
4	Laur. Traversanus. *Epitome margaritae eloquentiae.* [Caxton, after 21 January 1480] Cx 35, STC 24190.3. Leeds University, Brotherton Library.		?36	?5
5	[MS on paper:] Joh. Nider. *Expositio decalogi.* Imperfect.		16	?2

28. THOMAS TANNER. 4°. Disbound. Thomas Tanner (1674–1735), bishop of St. Asaph. By bequest, with many other printed books and MSS, to the Bodleian Library. Nos. 1 and 2 were originally in "a volume of black-letter tracts" (DeR), with former class-mark Tanner 178. The original order of contents is uncertain.

		LEAVES	QUIRES
1	*The Thre Kynges of Coleyn.* Wynkyn de Worde, [ca. 1496] Duff 397, Bodl. Tanner 178(1).	44	6
2	*Medytacions of Saynt Bernarde.* Wynkyn de Worde, 9 March 1496. Duff 41, Bodl. Tanner 178(2).	32	5
3	*The Governal of Health.* [1490] Cx 99, Duff 165, DeR 47.2, Bodl. Arch. G.f.10.	18	3
4	*Ars moriendi,* Eng. [1491] Cx 109, Duff 33, DeR 5.1, Bodl. Arch. G.f.9.	8	1
5	*King Salomon & Marcolphus.* Antwerp: G. Leeu, [ca. 1492] Duff 115, CA 460.	18	4

29. DURHAM CATHEDRAL. 4°. Disbound. Order of texts in original binding unknown.

		LEAVES	QUIRES
1	*The Book of Divers Ghostly Matters.* [1491] Cx 108, Duff 55, DeR 12.4.	148	19
2	*Cordiale of the Four Last Things.* Wynykn de Worde, [?ca. 1496–98] Duff 110.	92	12
3	*Rote of Consolation.* Wynkyn de Worde, [before 8 January 1498] Duff 364. (NB: the only surviving copy, lacking final 17 leaves.)	64	9

30. JOSEPH LILLY. F°. Disbound. Joseph Lilly, London bookseller, early nineteenth century. "Discovered . . . in a volume of old Law Tracts, among which, also, was an unique Machlinia" (Blades 2, 213). Sold to Thomas Grenville, and now in the British Library. There is no unique law book printed by Machlinia, but his editions of *Yearbook 34 Henry VI* (Duff 419), *Yearbook 37 Henry VI* (Duff 422), and *Statutes 1 Richard III* (Duff 379) are all rare, and are possible candidates as one of the other editions in this volume.

		LEAVES	QUIRES
1	*Statutes 1, 3, 4 Henry VII.* [1491]	42	5
	Cx 102, Duff 380, DeR 93.2, BL G.6002.		
2, etc.	Unidentified.	?	?

31. TRIPHOOK. F°. Disbound. Robert Triphook, London bookseller, early nineteenth century. Sold to Earl Spencer: "His Lordship obtained this copy from Mr. Triphook in a volume of old Tracts for £3 3s, but on verifying this as a Caxton made him a present of 50 guineas" (Blades 2, 213).

		LEAVES	QUIRES
1	*Statutes 1, 3, 4 Henry VII.* [1491]	42	5
	Cx 102, Duff 380, DeR 93.3.		
2, etc.	Unidentified.	?	?

32. INNER TEMPLE. F°. Intact.

		LEAVES	QUIRES
1	*Statutes 1, 3, 4 Henry VII.* [1491]	42	5
	Cx 102, Duff 380, DeR 93.1.		
2	T. Littleton. *Tenores novelli.* Rouen: Guill. Le Talleur f. R. Pynson. [?ca. 1493]	42	7
	Duff 275, Goff L-234.		

33. SAMUEL GRICE. 4°. Intact. Samuel Grice, unidentified, gave the volume in 1721 to George Oldham. It was acquired later by the British Museum.

		LEAVES	QUIRES
1	*Festum transfigurationis Iesu Christi.* [1487]	10	2
	Cx 86, Duff 146, DeR 42.1, BL IB.55122.		
2	*Festum dulcissimi nominis Iesu.* Pynson, [ca. 1493]	24	3
	Duff 143, BL IA.55557.		
3	Augustinus. *De virtute psalmorum.* [Antwerp:] M. van der Goes, [ca. 1490]	10	1
	CA 200, BMC IX 180 (IA.49899).		
4	Albertus Magnus. *De virtutibus animae.* Antwerp: G. Leeu, 14 March 1489.	32	5
	CA 77, BMC IX 192 (IA.49797).		
5	Joh. Nider. *De morali lepra.* [Louvain:] Joh. de Westfalia, [ca. 1490]	90	11
	CA 1287, BMC IX 156 (IA.49279).		

34. BISHOP MOORE. F°. Disbound, dispersed. Former ULC shelfmark AB.10.52. No. 3 remained at Cambridge University Library. No. 2 was sold in 1862 to Boone, later belonged to H. Huth, and is now in the Huntington Library. No. 1 was sold in 1870 to F. S. Ellis, and is apparently the copy later belonging to H. Huth, now in the Huntington Library.

		LEAVES	QUIRES
1	W. Hylton. *Scala perfectionis*. Wynkyn de Worde, 1494.	149	20
	Duff 203, ?Mead 5254 (ex-Huth, sale, 17 June 1913, lot 3694).		
2	*The Royal Book.* [1485–86]	162	20
	Cx 83, Duff 366, DeR 89.3, Mead 5241.		
3	*The Doctrinal of Sapience.* After 7 May 1489.	92	11
	Cx 94, Duff 127, DeR 40.2, Oates 4106.		

35. PICKERING. 4°. Disbound. William Pickering, London bookseller. This volume, "containing also some tracts printed by Wynkyn de Worde," was purchased by the British Museum, 1851, and there disbound.

		LEAVES	QUIRES
1	*The Fifteen Oes.* [1491]	22	3
	Cx 105, Duff 150, DeR 44.1.		
2, etc.	Unidentified.	?	?

36. FRANCIS BLOMEFIELD. F°. Intact. Francis Blomefield of Fersfield, Norfolk (1705–1752). The volume later belonged to Richard Warner of Woodford Row, Essex (?1713–1775), and was given by him to Wadham College, Oxford, shelf-mark A.6.11.

		LEAVES	QUIRES
1	Boethius. *The Consolation of Philosophy.* [1478]	94	12
	Cx 31, Duff 47, DeR 8.16, Rhodes 402(c).		
2	Bonaventura. *Speculum vitae Christi*, Eng. R. Pynson, [1494]	124	17
	Duff 51, Rhodes 413.		

37. R. JOHNSON. F°. Disbound. Cambridge University Library, formerly in Bishop Moore's library. Assembled by R. Johnson, in 1510, with notes of the prices he paid for each copy. The signature of Edmund Smithe appears in no. 1. Three other volumes with R. Johnson's dated ownership inscriptions are known, acquired 1503, 1520, and 1523 (see A. I. Doyle in *Notes and Queries* 1952: 293–94).

		LEAVES	QUIRES
1	*Godfrey of Boloyne.* 20 November 1481.	144	19
	Cx 48, Duff 164, DeR 46.5, Oates 4079.		
	Price: 2s.		
2	*The Book of Eneydos.* After 22 June 1490.	86	12
	Cx 97, Duff 404, DeR 96.1, Oates 4108.		
	Price: 12d.		
3	Christine de Pisan. *Fayts of Arms.* 14 July 1489.	144	19
	Cx 90, Duff 96, DeR 28.6, Oates 4107.		
	Price: 2s. 8d.		
4	*The Chastising of God's Children.* [Wynkyn de Worde, ca. 1492]	48	9
	Duff 85, DeR 104.2, Oates 4115.		
	Price: 8d.		
5	G. Chaucer. *The Book of Fame.* [1483]	30	4
	Cx 59, Duff 86, DeR 21.4, Oates 4094.		
	Price: 4d.		

Appendix C

Binder's Waste and Caxton's Printing

THE FOLLOWING LIST does not include all examples of Caxton's printing found as binder's waste but only those items surviving solely through their preservation in bindings.

Countless bibliographical studies have drawn on evidence from binder's waste. A useful general study of printed waste is Konrad Haebler, "Makulatorforschung," in *Zentralblatt für Bibliothekswesen* 25 (1908), 535–44. There is a classic monograph on manuscript waste in the book trade of one city by Neil R. Ker, *Fragments of Medieval Manuscripts Used as Pastedowns in Oxford Bindings* (Oxford, 1954).

1. Rounceval Indulgence, [ca. 1480]. Broadside. Cx 44.
   SOURCE: A now-lost Caxton binding covering four folio editions printed by Caxton, formerly Lessing Rosenwald's, now Library of Congress (Tract Vol. 8).

2. Rhodes Indulgence, 1480. Broadside. Singular issue, counterpart to the plural issue, no. 3 below. Cx 42.
   SOURCE: An Oxford binding covering Lathbury *Super opus threnorum*, [Oxford], 31 July 1482, F°, Duff 238, formerly Simon Pottesman's, sold Sotheby's, 16 October 1979, lot 253, now British Library. Dr. Christopher de Hamel of Sotheby's has since discovered four more bindings from this Oxford shop likewise variously containing, as quire guards, cut-up strips of these two Caxton printings (Cx 42 and 43), and also of one Johann Lettou printing (Duff 208) of the 1480 Rhodes indulgence.

3. Rhodes Indulgence, 1480. Broadside. Plural issue, counterpart to the singular issue, no. 2 above. Cx 43, Duff 207.
   SOURCES: (*a*) Several Oxford bindings, cf. no. 2 above; (*b*) binding on the 1499–1500 Accounts of King's Hall (now Trinity College), Cambridge.

4. Rhodes Indulgence, 1481. Broadside. Singular issue. Cx 50, Duff 209.
   SOURCES: (*a*) Caxton binding on *The Royal Book* [Caxton, ca. 1485–86], F°, Cx 83, Duff 366, DeR 89.1, now in the Pierpont Morgan Library, Nixon List 14; (*b*) Caxton binding on Gower, *Confessio amantis*, Caxton, 2 September 1483, Cx 66, Duff 166, now at the University of North Carolina, Nixon List 12; (*c*) ?now-lost Caxton binding on J. Nider, *Sermones de tempore* [Esslingen: C. Fyner, ca. 1477], F°, Goff N-215, at King's College, Cambridge (cf. Chawner 33 and 182). A strip of four lines, preserved as a quire guard. The binding of the Nider is eighteenth century, and the strip is presumably a remnant of the original binding.

5. Rhodes Indulgence, 1481. Broadside. Plural issue. Cx 49, Duff 210.
   SOURCES: (*a*) Destroyed Caxton binding formerly covering a copy of Boethius, *The Consolation of Philosophy* [Caxton, 1478], F°, Cx 31, Duff 47, DeR 8.8, whose pasteboards were made up of a large quantity of waste sheets from thirteen different pieces of Caxton's printing; the Boethius itself, in a

modern binding, is now in the Library of Congress as part of the Rosenwald gift; Nixon List 6; (*b*) empty Caxton binding at Durham Cathedral, formerly containing six folio incunables printed at Venice, Cologne, and Ghent, 1482–83; Nixon List 13; (*c*) ?fragments of undetermined source, in Lincoln College, Oxford, listed by Duff 210, but no longer to be found (see Rhodes, p. xiv).

6. Sarum *Ordinal*, [1477]. 4°. Cx 23, Duff 336. Fragments only: eight leaves.
   SOURCE: The destroyed Caxton binding listed 5(*a*) above.

7. Sarum *Hours*, [ca. 1477–79]. 4°. Cx 33, Duff 175. Fragments only: four leaves, probably trial printing.
   SOURCE: The destroyed Caxton binding listed 5(*a*) above.

8. Advertisement for Sarum *Ordinal*, [1477]. Broadside. Cx 24, Duff 80.
   SOURCE: Presumably binder's waste. Both surviving copies were owned by Francis Douce. He gave one to Earl Spencer, who had it bound into his copy of the first edition of *Dicts of Philosophers*: see A. N. L. Munby, *Connoisseurs and Medieval Miniatures, 1750–1850* (Oxford, 1972), 49.

9. Lydgate, *The Life of Our Lady*, [1483]. F°. Cx 62, Duff 266a. Fragments only: sheets a 2.7 and 3.6. Probably trial printing related to Caxton's completed edition of the same text, Duff 266.
   SOURCES: (*a*) Caxton binding formerly covering (but now separated from) a copy of Boethius, *The Consolation of Philosophy* [Caxton, 1478], F°, Cx 31, Duff 47, DeR 8.29, in the St. Bride's Printing Library, London; Nixon List 5. (*b*) The Douce example of these fragments, Bodl. Douce frag. d. 3, apparently has a different provenance, being noted as "found within the worm eaten cover of Caxton's Cicero de Amicicia" (i.e., Cx 45, Duff 103). This copy of Cicero cannot be identified; Douce himself is not known to have owned a copy.

10–11. Two Sarum *Hours*, [ca. 1491], one 4°, one 8°. Cx 106–7.
   SOURCE: Caxton binding covering a copy of Caxton's 2d edition of *Mirror of the World* [1489], F°, Cx 95, Duff 402, DeR 95.7, formerly at Bristol Baptist College, now in the British Library; Nixon List 16. The printer's waste in this volume belongs to Caxton's edition of the *Fifteen Oes* [1491], 4°, Cx 105, Duff 150, a book which also survives in a complete copy at the British Library. But offsetting on the Bristol Baptist College waste leaves was identified by G. D. Painter as belonging to two otherwise unrecorded Books of Hours, one in octavo and one in quarto format: see his "Caxton through the Looking Glass" in *Gutenberg Jahrbuch* 1963: 73–80, a classic of bibliographical detection.

12. Sarum *Hours*, [ca. 1484]. 8°. Cx 77, Duff 178–79. Fragments only: 12 leaves.
   SOURCE: An unidentified binding. The fragments, consisting of sheet m and leaves d1–4, were presented to the British Museum in 1858 by William Maskell.

13. Donatus, [ca. 1484–87]. F°. Cx 78, Duff 129. Fragments of a single bifolium, printed on vellum.
   SOURCE: An unidentified binding at New College, Oxford. Discovered there in 1893 by Robert Proctor. See Rhodes 701 and pl. 5.

At least three more volumes bound in Caxton's bindery (Nixon List 21, 22, 27) also contain or once contained printer's waste, including fragments of an otherwise unrecorded octavo Sarum *Hours* printed by Wynkyn de Worde, ca. 1494 (Duff 185).

Appendix D

Checklist of Caxton's Printing

THE LIST includes Caxton's printing in Cologne, Bruges, and Westminster and the two service books printed for him in Paris. The Cologne shop was that of the so-called Printer of Dares, Johann Schilling; there is adequate evidence to show that in 1472 this shop was working exclusively for Caxton. I have omitted the two "Image of Pity" woodcuts, DeR 54 (STC 14077c.6, Hodnett 381) and 55 (STC 14077c.8, Hodnett 380), on the grounds that they are not typography, are not publications, and are only dubiously connected with Caxton's shop. Blades citations not enclosed in parentheses refer to the list in volume 2 of *The Life and Typography of William Caxton*, London, 1861–63. Citations within parentheses refer to the list in Blades's abridgment, *The Biography and Typography of William Caxton*, London, 1877, insofar as it differs from the 1863 list. A revised second edition of the *Biography* was published in 1882, with the same numbering as the 1877 list.

COLOGNE

Cx 1
Bartholomaeus Anglicus. *De proprietatibus rerum*. [1472]
Royal F°. [1–24¹⁰ 25⁸]: 248 leaves. Veldener's Cologne type.
Duff 39, Goff B-131, Hain 2498, VK 218, GW 3403.

Cx 2
Gesta romanorum. [1472]
F°. [1–12¹⁰]: 120 leaves. Veldener's Cologne type.
Goff G-281, Hain 7738, VK 501.

Cx 3
Walter Burley. *De vita et moribus philosophorum*. [1472]
F°. [1–4¹⁰ 5⁸ 6¹⁰]: 58 leaves. Veldener's Cologne type.
Goff B-1318, Hain 4113, VK 296, GW 5784.

BRUGES

Cx 4
Raoul Le Fèvre. *Recuyell of the Histories of Troy*, tr. William Caxton. [1473–74]
F°. [1–13¹⁰ 14⁸; 15–23¹⁰ 24–25⁸; 26–35¹⁰]: 352 leaves. Type 1.
Duff 242, DeR 3, Blades 1, STC 15375, Goff L-117, Hain 7048, CA(I) 1093A.

Cx 5
Jacobus de Cessolis. *The Game and Play of Chess*[1], tr. William Caxton. 31 March 1474.
F°. [1–8⁸ 9¹⁰]: 74 leaves. Type 1.
Duff 81, DeR 1, Blades 2 (3), STC 4920, Goff C-413, Hain 4902, GW 6532, CA(I) 418A.

Cx 6
Raoul Le Fèvre. *Recueil des histoires de Troie*. [ca. 1474]
F°. [1–12¹⁰; 13–20¹⁰ 21⁶; 22–29¹⁰]: 286 leaves. Type 1.
Duff 243, DeR 3b, Blades 3 (2), Goff L-113, Hain 7042, CA(I) 1093B.

Cx 7
Pierre d'Ailly. *Meditationes circa psalmos penitentiales*, French. [ca. 1475]
F°. [1–3⁸ 4¹⁰]: 34 leaves. Type 1.
Duff 25, DeR 3d, Blades 5, Cop. 385, CA 147.

Cx 8
Gerard of Vliederhoven. *Cordiale quattuor novissimorum*, French, tr. Jean Mielot. [ca. 1475]
F°. [1–4⁸ 5¹⁰; 6–9⁸]: 74 leaves. Type 2.
Duff 108, DeR 2, Blades 6, Goff C-908, Cop. 1797, GW 7530, CA(I) 423A.

Cx 9
Raoul Le Fèvre. *Histoire de Jason*. [ca. 1476]
F°. [1–16⁸ 17⁶]: 134 leaves. Type 1.

Duff 244, DeR 3c, Blades 4, Hain 7050, CA(I) 1090A.
Note: Printed in Bruges with type 1 after Caxton had
removed to Westminster with type 2, ca. 1475–76.

WESTMINSTER

Cx 10
John Russell. *Propositio.* [before September 1476]
4° (half sheets). [1⁴]: 4 leaves. Type 2.
Duff 367, DeR 90, Blades 7 (12), STC 21548, Hain 14048.
Cited: Tract Vol. 6 (Cx 10 + 37 + non-Caxton material).

Cx 11
Sarum *Hours.* [1476]
8° (half sheets). Quired in 8s; total of leaves unknown.
Type 2.
Duff 174, DeR 50, Blades 11 (9), STC 15867, Goff H-420,
Cop. 3052.
Note: Possibly printed in Bruges, but more probably, in light
of its half-sheet format, an early Westminster production.

Cx 12
Cato. *Disticha¹*, Latin-English, tr. Benedict Burgh. [1476]
4° (half sheets). [1–3⁸ 4¹⁰]: 34 leaves. Type 2.
Duff 77, DeR 14, Blades 16 (15), STC 4851, Goff C-314,
Cop. 1530, GW 6359.
Cited: Tract Vol. 2 (Cx 12 + 15).

Cx 13
John Lydgate. *The Churl and the Bird¹.* [1476]
4° (half sheets). [1¹⁰]: 10 leaves. Type 2.
Duff 257, DeR 67, Blades 21, STC 17009, Goff L-406,
Cop. 3701.
Cited: Tract Vol. 1 (Cx 13 + 14 + non-Caxton material).

Cx 14
John Lydgate. *The Horse, the Sheep and the Goose¹.* [1476]
4° (half sheets). [1⁸ 2¹⁰]: 18 leaves. Type 2.
Duff 262, DeR 70, Blades 18 (17), STC 17019, Goff L-407,
Cop. 3698.
Cited: Tract Vol. 1 (Cx 13 + 14 + non-Caxton material).

Cx 15
John Lydgate. *Stans puer ad mensam*, English. [?1476]
4° (half sheets). [1⁴]: 4 leaves. Type 2.
Duff 269, DeR 74, Blades 14 (13), STC 17030, Goff L-411,
Hain 4927 (pts. 1–2).
Cited: Tract Vols. 3 (Cx 15 + 18 + 19 + 21 + 22 + 27 +
28 + 29); 2 (Cx 12 + 15).

Cx 16
Indulgence. Extension to England of the 1475 Rome Jubilee
indulgence: John Sant, abbot of Abingdon, commissary.
[before 13 December] 1476.
Broadside. Types 2, 3.
STC 14077 c.106.
Cited: p. 32 and notes, p. 57.

Cx 17
Geoffrey Chaucer. *The Canterbury Tales* [1477]
F°. [1–32⁸ 33¹⁰; 34–39⁸ 40⁶; 41–46⁸ 47⁶]: 374 leaves. Type 2.
Duff 87, DeR 22, Blades 12 (10), STC 5082, Goff C-431,
Hain 4921, GW 6585.
Cited: See fig. 10 (p. 38).

Cx 18
John Lydgate. *The Horse, the Sheep and the Goose².* [1477]
4° (half sheets). [1⁸ 2¹⁰]: 18 leaves. Type 2.
Duff 261, DeR 69, Blades 17 (16), STC 17018, Hain 4927
(pts. 6–7).
Cited: Tract Vol. 3 (Cx 15 + 18 + 19 + 21 + 22 + 27 +
28 + 29).

Cx 19
John Lydgate. *The Churl and the Bird².* [1477]
4° (half sheets). [1¹⁰]: 10 leaves. Type 2.
Duff 256, DeR 66, Blades 20, STC 17008, Hain 4927 (pt. 5).
Cited: Tract Vol. 3 (Cx 15 + 18 + 19 + 21 + 22 + 27 +
28 + 29).

Cx 20
Infancia salvatoris. [1477]
4° (half sheets). [1⁸ 2¹⁰]: 18 leaves. Type 2.
Duff 222, DeR 62, Blades 8 (18), STC 14551, Goff I-73,
Hain 9180.
Cited: Tract Vol. 4 (Cx 20 + non-Caxton material).

Cx 21
John Lydgate. *The Temple of Glass.* [1477]
4° (half sheets). [1–3⁸ 4¹⁰]: 34 leaves. Type 2.
Duff 270, DeR 75, Blades 19, STC 17032, Hain 4927 (pt. 8).
Cited: Tract Vol. 3 (Cx 15 + 18 + 19 + 21 + 22 + 27 +
28 + 29).

Cx 22
Cato. *Disticha²*, Latin-English, tr. Benedict Burgh. [1477]
4° (half sheets). [1–3⁸ 4¹⁰]: 34 leaves. Type 2.
Duff 76, DeR 13, Blades 15 (14), STC 4850, Hain 4927 (pts.
3–4), GW 6358.
Cited: Tract Vol. 3 (Cx 15 + 18 + 19 + 21 + 22 + 27 +
28 + 29).

Cx 23
Sarum *Ordinal.* [1477]

4°. Quired in 8s: total of leaves unknown. Type 3.
Duff 336, DeR 82, Blades 36, STC 16228, Cop. 4496.
Cited: Bdr's Waste 6.

Cx 24
Advertisement for Sarum *Ordinal*. [1477]
Broadside (quarter sheet). Type 3.
Duff 80, DeR 17, Blades 35, STC 4890, Cop. 32, GW 6440, *Einbl.* 479.
Cited: Bdr's Waste 8.

Cx 25
Raoul Le Fevre. *The History of Jason*, tr. William Caxton. [1477]
F°. [1–18⁸ 19⁶]: 150 leaves. Type 2.
Duff 245, DeR 64, Blades 9 (7), STC 15383, Goff L-112, Hain 7053.

Cx 26
Dicts and Sayings of the Philosophers[1]. Tr. Anthony Woodville, Earl Rivers. [before] 18 November 1477.
F°. [1–9⁸ 10⁶]: 78 leaves. Type 2.
Duff 123, DeR 36–37, Blades 10 (8), STC 6826–27, Goff D-272, Hain 6284, GW 8321.
Cited: Tract Vol. 5 (Cx 26 + 30); and see pp. 23–24.

Cx 27
Geoffrey Chaucer. *The Temple of Brass* (i.e., *The Parlement of Fowls*). [1477]
4° (half sheets). [1–3⁸ + ?]: 24 (+ ?) leaves. Type 2.
Duff 93, DeR 25, Blades 22, STC 5091, Hain 4927 (pts. 9–11), GW 6591.
Cited: Tract Vol. 3 (Cx 15 + 18 + 19 + 21 + 22 + 27 + 28 + 29).

Cx 28
Geoffrey Chaucer. *Queen Anelida and the False Arcite*. [1477]
4° (half sheets). [1¹⁰]: 10 leaves. Type 2.
Duff 92, DeR 24, Blades 24, STC 5090, Hain 4927 (pts. 13–15), GW 6584.
Cited: Tract Vol. 3 (Cx 15 + 18 + 19 + 21 + 22 + 27 + 28 + 29).

Cx 29
The Book of Courtesy. [1477]
4° (half sheets). [1⁸ 2⁶]: 14 leaves. Type 2.
Duff 53, DeR 11, Blades 23, STC 3303, Hain 4927 (pt. 12).
Cited: Tract Vol. 3 (Cx 15 + 18 + 19 + 21 + 22 + 27 + 28 + 29).

Cx 30
Christine de Pisan. *Moral Proverbs*, tr. Anthony Woodville, Earl Rivers. 20 February 1478.
F°. [1⁴]: 4 leaves. Type 2.
Duff 95, DeR 27, Blades 13 (11), STC 7273, Goff C-473,

Hain 4987, GW 6650.
Cited: Tract Vol. 5 (Cx 26 + 30).

Cx 31
Boethius. *The Consolation of Philosophy*, tr. Geoffrey Chaucer. [1478]
F°. [1–11⁸ 12⁶]: 94 leaves. Types 2, 3.
Duff 47, DeR 8, Blades 25, STC 3199, Goff B-813, Hain 3399, GW 4576.
Cited: Tract Vols. 7 (Cx 31 + 41); 11 (Cx 31 + 63 + 68 + non-Caxton material); 16 (Cx 31 + 68 + 69 + 70); 36 (Cx 31 + non-Caxton material); and see Bdr's Waste 5 and 9.

Cx 32
Laurentius Traversanus. *Nova rhetorica sive Margarita eloquentiae*. [after 26 July 1478]
F°. [1–12¹⁰ 13⁶]: 126 leaves. Type 2*.
Duff 368, DeR 91, Blades 27, STC 24188.5 = 24189, Cop. 5270.

Cx 33
Sarum *Hours*. [ca. 1477–79]
4°. 4 leaves survive; probably trial printing. There is no evidence for whether this resulted in a completed edition. Type 3.
Duff 175, DeR 51, Blades 37, STC 15868, Cop. 3131.
Cited: Bdr's Waste 7.

Cx 34
Gerard of Vliederhoven. *Cordiale quattuor novissimorum*, English, tr. Anthony Woodville, Earl Rivers. 24 March 1479.
F°. [1–9⁸ 10⁶]: 78 leaves. Types 2*, 3.
Duff 109, DeR 33, Blades 26, STC 5758, Goff C-907, Hain 5714, GW 7536.
Cited: Tract Vol. 8 (Cx 34 + 38 + 45 + 46 + 44 as binder's waste).

Cx 35
Laurentius Traversanus. *Epitome margaritae eloquentiae*. [after 21 January 1480]
F°. [?1–3⁸ 4–5⁶]: ?36 leaves. Type 2*.
STC 24190.3.
Cited: Tract Vol. 27 (Cx 35 + non-Caxton material).

Cx 36
Indulgence. For the Knights of Rhodes: John Kendale, commissary. Single issue. 1480 [before 31 March]
Broadside. Type 2*.
Duff 204, DeR 56, Blades 29, STC 14077 c.107 (formerly 22582), Cop. 5501 = 3447, *Einbl.* 820.
Cited: Headnote to Appendix A.

Cx 37
Officium visitationis BMV. [1480]
4°. [?1–3⁸]: ?24 leaves. Type 4.

Duff 148, DeR 43, Blades 49 (51), STC 15848, Cop. 5443.
Cited: Tract Vol. 6 (Cx 10 + 37 + non-Caxton material).

Cx 38

Dicts and Sayings of the Philosophers[2], tr. Anthony Wood-ville, Earl Rivers. "18 November 1477" [ca. June 1480]
F°. [1–9⁸ 10⁶]: 78 leaves. Type 2*.
Duff 124, DeR 38, Blades 28, STC 6828, Goff D-273, GW 8322.
Cited: Tract Vol. 8 (Cx 34 + 38 + 45 + 46 + 44 as binder's waste); and see pp. 23–24.

Cx 39

Chronicles of England[1]. 10 June 1480.
F°. π⁸; a–x⁸ y⁶: 182 leaves. Type 4.
Duff 97, DeR 29, Blades 39, STC 9991, Goff C-477 (pt. 1), Hain 5000 (pt. 1), GW 6670 (pt. 1).
Cited: Headnote to Appendix B.

Cx 40

Description of Britain. 18 August 1480.
F°. [1–3⁸ 4⁶]: 30 leaves. Type 4.
Duff 113, DeR 35, Blades 40, STC 13440 a, Goff C-477 (pt. 2), Hain 5000 (pt. 2), GW 6670 (pt. 2).
Cited: Headnote to Appendix B.

Cx 41

The Doctrine to Learn French and English. [1480]
F°. a–b⁸ c¹⁰: 26 leaves. Type 4.
Duff 405, DeR 97, Blades 46 (48), STC 24865, Goff v-315, Hain 15607.
Cited: Tract Vols. 7 (Cx 31 + 41); 14 (Cx 41 + 56 + 58).

Cx 42

Indulgence. For the Knights of Rhodes: John Kendale, commissary. Single issue. 1480.
Broadside. Type 4.
In the Addenda to STC² this will be given the number 14077 c.110A.
Cited: Bdr's Waste 2.

Cx 43

Indulgence. For the Knights of Rhodes: John Kendale, commissary. Plural issue. 1480.
Broadside. Type 4.
Duff 207, DeR 57, STC 14077 c.110 (formerly 22584), *Einbl.* 821.
Cited: Bdr's Waste 3.

Cx 44

Indulgence. Hospital of St. Mary Rounceval, Charing Cross: letter of confraternity: Edward Ponyngs, John Kendale, and John Lynton, proctors. Plural issue. [ca. 1480]
Broadside. Type 4.
In the Addenda to STC² this will be given the number 14077 c.55B.
Cited: Binder's waste in Tract Vol. 8 (Cx 34 + 38 + 44 + 45 + 46) = Bdr's Waste 1.

Cx 45

Cicero. *Of Old Age* (?tr. Stephen Scrope); Cicero. *Of Friendship*; and Bonacursius of Montemagno. *Of Nobility* (?both tr. John Tiptoft, earl of Worcester). 12 August [–ca. September] 1481.
F°. 1⁶; a⁶ b–h⁸ i⁴; ²a–²f⁸: 120 leaves. Types 2*, 3.
Duff 103, DeR 31, Blades 33, STC 5293, Goff c-627, Hain 5311, GW 6992.
Cited: Tract Vols. 8 (Cx 34 + 38 + 45 + 46 + 44 as binder's waste); 9 (Cx 45 + 46); and see Bdr's Waste 9.

Cx 46

The Mirror of the World, tr. William Caxton. After 8 March [ca. October] 1481.
F°. a–m⁸ n⁴: 100 leaves. Type 2*.
Duff 401, DeR 94, Blades 31, STC 24762, Goff M-883, Hain 11656.
Cited: Tract Vols. 8 (Cx 34 + 38 + 45 + 46 + 44 as binder's waste); 9 (Cx 45 + 46).

Cx 47

Psalterium cum canticis. [1481]
4°. a–u⁸ x⁸ (7+1) y⁸: 177 leaves. Type 3.
Duff 354, DeR 84, Blades 38, STC 16253, Cop. 4925.

Cx 48

Godfrey of Boloyne, tr. William Caxton. 20 November 1481.
F°. a⁶ b⁴; 1–16⁸ 17⁶: 144 leaves. Type 4.
Duff 164, DeR 46, Blades 42, STC 13175, Goff G-316, Hain 3684.
Cited: Tract Vol. 37 (Cx 48 + 59 + 90 + 97 + non-Caxton material).

Cx 49

Indulgence. For the Knights of Rhodes: Johannes de Gigliis, commissary. Plural issue. 1481.
Broadside. Type 4.
Duff 210, DeR 59, Blades 40* (43), STC 14077 c.113 (formerly 22587), Cop. 5506, *Einbl.* 797.
Cited: Bdr's Waste 5.

Cx 50

Indulgence. For the Knights of Rhodes: Johannes de Gigliis, commissary. Single issue. 1481.
Broadside. Type 4.
Duff 209, DeR 58, Blades (44), STC 14077 c.112 (formerly 22586), Goff s-565, Cop. 5507, *Einbl.* 796 = 14.
Cited: Bdr's Waste 4.

Cx 51

Reynard the Fox[1], tr. William Caxton. [1482]

F°. a–g⁸ h⁸ (8 + half leaf) i⁸ k–l⁶: 84 (+ ½) leaves. Type 2*.
Duff 358, DeR 87, Blades 32, STC 20919, Goff R-137, Hain 861.
Cited: Tract Vol. 10 (Cx 51 + 56 + 57 + 58 + 61 + 68).

Cx 52
Ranulph Higden. *Polycronicon*, tr. John Trevisa. After 2 July 1482.
F°. a–b⁸ c⁴; 1–28⁸ x²; 29–48⁸ 49⁴; 50⁸ 52–55⁸: 450 leaves. Type 4.
Duff 172, DeR 49, Blades 44 (46), STC 13438, Goff H-267, Hain 8659.

Cx 53
*Chronicles of England*². 8 October 1482.
F°. π⁸; a–x⁸y⁶: 182 leaves. Type 4.
Duff 98, DeR 30, Blades 43 (45), STC 9992, Goff C-478, Hain 5002, GW 6671.
Cited: Headnote to Appendix B.

Cx 54
*Quattuor sermones*¹ (in English). [1482–83]
F°. a–c⁸ d⁶: 30 leaves. Type 4*.
Duff 299, DeR 85, Blades 48 (50), STC 17957 (note), Hain 7029 (pt. 2).
Note: Hain, Blades, De Ricci, and Duff conflated or failed to distinguish between two closely similar editions; see also Cx 85 below.
Cited: Tract Vols. 12 (Cx 54 + 55 + 60 + non-Caxton material); 13 (Cx 54 + 59 + ?57); and headnote to Appendix B.

Cx 55
Geoffrey Chaucer. *The Canterbury Tales*². [1483]
F°. a–t⁸ v⁶; aa–hh⁸ ii⁶; A–K⁸ L⁶: 312 leaves. Types 2*, 4*.
Duff 88, DeR 23, Blades 57 (60), STC 5083, Goff C-432, Hain 4922, GW 6586.
Cited: Tract Vol. 12 (Cx 54 + 55 + 60 + non-Caxton material).

Cx 56
Cato. *Disticha*³, Latin-English, tr. Benedict Burgh. [1483]
F°. a–c⁸ d⁴: 28 leaves. Types 2*, 3.
Duff 78, DeR 15, Blades 30, STC 4852, Hain 4755, GW 6360.
Cited: Tract Vols. 10 (Cx 51 + 56 + 57 + 58 + 61 + 68); 14 (Cx 41 + 56 + 58); 26 (Cx 56 + 61 + 64 + 97 + non-Caxton material).

Cx 57
Jacobus de Cessolis. *The Game and Play of Chess*², tr. William Caxton. [1483]
F°. [a]⁸ b–i⁸ k–l⁶: 84 leaves. Type 2*.
Duff 82, DeR 18, Blades 34, STC 4921, Goff C-414, Hain

4901, GW 6533.
Cited: Tract Vols. 10 (Cx 51 + 56 + 57 + 58 + 61 + 68); 13 (Cx 54 + 59 + ?57); 22 (Cx 57 + 90).

Cx 58
Alain Chartier. *Le Curial*, tr. William Caxton. [1483]
F°. [1⁶]: 6 leaves. Type 4*.
Duff 84, DeR 20, Blades 59 (62), STC 5057, Goff C-429, Hain 4918, GW 6563.
Cited: Tract Vols. 10 (Cx 51 + 56 + 57 + 58 + 61 + 68); 14 (Cx 41 + 56 + 58); 15 (Cx 58 + 59 + 73 + 97).

Cx 59
Geoffrey Chaucer. *The Book of Fame*. [1483]
F°. a–c⁸ d⁶: 30 leaves. Type 4*.
Duff 86, DeR 21, Blades 58 (61), STC 5087, Hain 4925, GW 6589.
Cited: Tract Vols. 13 (Cx 54 + 59 + ?57); 15 (Cx 58 + 59 + 73 + 97); 37 (Cx 48 + 59 + 90 + 97 + non-Caxton material).

Cx 60
Geoffrey Chaucer. *Troilus and Criseyde*. [1483]
F°. a–g⁸ h¹⁰; i–o⁸ p⁶: 120 leaves. Type 4*.
Duff 94, DeR 26, Blades 60 (63), STC 5094, Hain 4926, GW 6592.
Cited: Tract Vol. 12 (Cx 54 + 55 + 60 + non-Caxton material).

Cx 61
The Court of Sapience. [1483]
F°. a–e⁸: 40 leaves. Type 4.
Duff 260, DeR 68, Blades 41, STC 17015, Hain 10353.
Cited: Tract Vols. 10 (Cx 51 + 56 + 57 + 58 + 61 + 68); 26 (Cx 56 + 61 + 64 + 97 + non-Caxton material).

Cx 62
John Lydgate. *The Life of Our Lady*. [1483]
F°. a 2.7, 3.6 only; apparently trial printing: 4 leaves. Type 4*.
Duff 266a, DeR 72, STC 17024, Goff L-410.
Cited: Bdr's Waste 9.

Cx 63
John Lydgate. *The Life of Our Lady*. [1483]
F°. π²; a–l⁸: 96 leaves. Type 4*.
Duff 266, DeR 71, Blades 61 (64), STC 17023, Goff L-409, Hain 10352.
Cited: Tract Vol. 11 (Cx 31 + 63 + 68 + non-Caxton material).

Cx 64
Guillaume de Deguilleville. *The Pilgrimage of the Soul*. 6 June 1483.
F°. π⁴; a–n⁸ o⁶: 114 leaves. Type 4.
Duff 267, DeR 73, Blades 45 (47), STC 6473–74, Goff

G-640, Hain 8331.
Cited: Tract Vols. 24 (Cx 64 + 74 + 98); 26 (Cx 56 + 61 + 64 + 97 + non-Caxton material).

Cx 65
John Mirk. *Festial*[1]. 30 June 1483.
F°. a–n[8] o–p[6]: 116 leaves. Type 4*.
Duff 298, DeR 79, Blades 47 (49), STC 17957 (pt. 1), Goff M-620, Hain 7029 (pt. 1).
Cited: Headnote to Appendix B.

Cx 66
John Gower. *Confessio amantis*, English. 2 September 1483.
Median F°. π^6; 1[8]b–z[8] &[8] A–B[8] C[6]: 220 leaves. Types 4, 4*.
Duff 166, DeR 48, Blades 50 (53), STC 12142, Goff G-329, Hain 7835.
Cited: See Bdr's Waste 4.

Cx 67
Jacobus de Voragine. *The Golden Legend*, tr. William Caxton. 20 November 1483.
Royal F°. [*A* copies:] π^6; a–z &[8] ɔ[6]; A–V[8] X[6] Y[2] (2+1); aa–ff[8]. gg[6] hh–ii[8] kk[6]. [*B* copies:] π^4; a–z &[8] ɔ[6]; A–X[8]; aa–ff[8] gg[6]. hh–ii[8] kk[6]: 449 [*A* copies] or 446 [*B* copies] leaves. Types 3, 4* [*A* copies] or 3, 4*, 5 [*B* copies].
Duff 408–9, DeR 98–99, Blades 53, 66 (56, 69), STC 24873–74, Goff J-148–49, Cop. 6472–73.
Note: Quires a–t and A–E of *The Golden Legend* exist in a single setting. The remaining quires are known in duplicate settings. One setting [*A*] of these quires has the same layout as the common quires a–t and A–E, using type 3 for the headlines. The other setting [*B*] used type 5 for the headlines. Most copies consist of either only *A*-settings or only *B*-settings for these duplicated quires, but a few copies contain mixtures of *A*- and *B*-quires. There is good reason to believe that the duplicate settings were produced concurrently.

Cx 68
Cato. *Disticha*, tr. William Caxton. [1484]
F°. π^4; a–h[8] i[10]: 80 leaves. Types 2*, 4*.
Duff 79, DeR 16, Blades 52 (55), STC 4853, Goff C-313, Hain 4754, GW 6361.
Cited: Tract Vols. 10 (Cx 51 + 56 + 57 + 58 + 61 + 68); 11 (Cx 31 + 63 + 68 + non-Caxton material); 16 (Cx 31 + 68 + 69 + 70); and see 21.

Cx 69
Geoffroy de La Tour-Landry. *The Knight of the Tower*, tr. William Caxton. 31 January 1484.
F°. π^4; a–m[8] n[6]: 106 leaves. Types 4, 4*.
Duff 241, DeR 63, Blades 51 (54), STC 15296, Goff L-72, Hain 9784.

Cited: Tract Vol. 16 (Cx 31 + 68 + 69 + 73).

Cx 70
Aesop. *Fables*, tr. William Caxton. 26 March 1484.
F°. a–s[8]: 144 leaves. Types 3, 4*.
Duff 4, DeR 4, Blades 55 (58), STC 175, Hain 360, GW 376.
Cited: Tract Vol. 16 (Cx 31 + 68 + 69 + 70).

Cx 71
The Order of Chivalry, tr. William Caxton. [1484]
4°. a–f[8] g[4]: 52 leaves. Types 3, 4*.
Duff 58, DeR 81, Blades 56 (59), STC 3326, Goff O-93, Hain 12077.
Cited: Tract Vol. 17 (Cx 71 + non-Caxton material).

Cx 72
Sixtus IV. *Sex quam elegantissimae epistolae*, ed. Petrus Carmelianus. [1484]
4°. a–c[8]: 24 leaves. Types 3, 4*.
Duff 371, DeR 92, Blades (52), STC 22588, Cop. 1457 = 5538.
Note: The unique surviving copy, now in the British Library, was discovered in Halberstadt in a volume of seventeenth-century tracts.

Cx 73
[Robert, abbot of Shrewsbury]. *The Life of St. Winifred*, tr. William Caxton. [1484]
F°. a–b[8]: 16 leaves. Type 4*.
Duff 414, DeR 100, Blades 62 (65), STC 25853, Goff w-62, Cop. 6583.
Cited: Tract Vol. 15 (Cx 58 + 59 + 73 + 97).

Cx 74
Deathbed Prayers. [?1484]
Broadside (half sheet). Types 3, 4*.
Duff 112, DeR 34, Blades 54 (57), STC 14554, Cop. 4838, *Einbl.* 509.
Cited: Tract Vol. 24 (Cx 64 + 74 + 98).

Cx 75
Pseudo-Bonaventure, i.e., Johannes de Caulibus. *Speculum vitae Christi*[1], English, tr. Nicholas Love. [ca. 1484]
F°. a–s[8] t[4]: 148 leaves. Type 5.
Duff 48, DeR 9, Blades 70 (71), STC 3259, Cop. 1178, GW 4763.

Cx 76
Clement Maydeston. *Directorium sacerdotum*[1]. [ca. 1484]
F°. π^6; a–q[8] r[10] s–t[8]: 160 leaves. Type 5.
Duff 290, DeR 77, Blades 69 (72), STC 17720, Hain 6271.

Cx 77
Sarum *Hours*. [ca. 1484]
8°. Quired in 8s; total of leaves unknown. Type 5.

Duff 178–79, DeR 52–53, Blades 72 (73, 80), STC 15871–72, Cop. 3128, 3130.
Cited: See Bdr's Waste 12. These two fragments have traditionally been treated as representing separate editions, but it is more likely that both belong to a single edition.

Cx 78
Donatus. *Ars minor*, ed. Antonius Mancinellus ("Donatus melior"). [ca. 1484–87]
F°. ?a^8 b^4: ?12 leaves. Type 5.
Duff 129, DeR 41, STC 7013, Cop. 3801, Rhodes 701, GW 9001.
Cited: See Bdr's Waste 13.

Cx 79
Indulgence. Dominican Priory of Arundel, Sussex: letter of confraternity: John Arundel, proctor. Plural issue. 1485.
Broadside. Type 4*.
Cited: See p. 45. Found by Dr. David Rogers in the Warwickshire Public Record Office, and as yet unpublished. In the Addenda to STC^2 it will be given the number 14077 c.25A.

Cx 80
Sir Thomas Malory. *Le Morte d'Arthur*. 31 July 1485.
F°. π–2π^8 3π^2; a–z & A–Z aa–dd^8 ee^6: 432 leaves. Type 4*.
Duff 283, DeR 76, Blades 63 (66), STC 801, Goff M-103, Hain 1864.

Cx 81
The History of Charles the Great, tr. William Caxton. 1 December 1485.
F°. a–m^8: 96 leaves. Type 4*.
Duff 83, DeR 19, Blades 64 (67), STC 5013, Hain 4521.
Cited: Tract Vol. 18 (Cx 81 + 82).

Cx 82
[Pierre de La Cépède]. *Paris and Vienne*, tr. William Caxton. 19 December 1485.
F°. a–c^8 d–e^6: 36 leaves. Type 4*.
Duff 337, DeR 83, Blades 65 (68), STC 19206, Cop. 4605.
Cited: Tract Vol. 18 (Cx 81 + 82), and see notes, p. 57.

Cx 83
Frère Laurent. *The Royal Book*, tr. William Caxton. [1485–86]
F°. a–t^8 u^{10}: 162 leaves. Type 5.
Duff 366, DeR 89, Blades 67 (74), STC 21429, Goff L-91, Hain 3691 = 14049.
Cited: Tract Vols. 19 (Cx 83 + 84 + 93 + 94); 20 (Cx 83 + 84 + 94); 23 (Cx 83 + ?94); 34 (Cx 83 + 94 + non-Caxton material); and see also Bdr's Waste 4.

Cx 84
Jacques Le Grand. *The Book of Good Manners*, tr. William

Caxton. 11 May 1487.
F°. a–g^8 h^{10}: 66 leaves. Type 5.
Duff 248, DeR 65, Blades 68 (70), STC 15394, Cop. 3754.
Cited: Tract Vols. 19 (Cx 83 + 84 + 93 + 94); 20 (Cx 83 + 84 + 94); 21 (Cx 84 + 93).

Cx 85
Quattuor Sermones^2, English. [1487]
F°. a–c^8 d^6: 30 leaves. Type 4*.
Duff 299, DeR 85, Blades 48 (50), STC 17957 (note), Goff Q-14, Hain 7029 (pt. 2).
Note: Hain, Blades, De Ricci, and Duff conflated or failed to distinguish between two closely similar editions; see also Cx 54 above.
Cited: Headnote to Appendix B.

Cx 86
Festum transfigurationis Iesu Christi. [1487]
4°. a^6 b^4: 10 leaves. Type 5.
Duff 146, DeR 42, Blades 73 (79), STC 15854, Cop. 5444.
Cited: Tract Vol. 33 (Cx 86 + non-Caxton material).

Cx 87
Commemoratio lamentationis BMV. [ca. 1487]
4°. a–d^8: 32 leaves. Type 5.
Duff 105, DeR 32, Blades (78), STC 17534, Cop. 1712.

Cx 88
Indulgence. On behalf of a campaign against the Turks: Johannes de Gigliis and Perseus de Malviciis, commissaries. Common issue. 1489 [before 24 April]
Broadside. Type 7.
Duff 211, DeR 60, STC 14077 c.114 (formerly 14100), Goff I-123, Cop. 3294, *Einbl.* 798.

Cx 89
Indulgence. On behalf of a campaign against the Turks: Johannes de Gigliis and Perseus de Malviciis, commissaries. Single issue. 1489.
Broadside. Type 7.
Duff 212, DeR 61, STC 14077 c.115 (formerly 14101), Cop. 3295, *Einbl.* 799.

Cx 90
Christine de Pisan. *Fayts of Arms*, tr. William Caxton. 14 July 1489.
F°. π^2; A–R^8 S^6: 144 leaves. Type 6.
Duff 96, DeR 28, Blades 74 (81), STC 7269, Goff C-472, Hain 4988 = 15918, GW 6648.
Cited: Tract Vols. 22 (Cx 57 + 90); 37 (Cx 48 + 59 + 90 + 97 + non-Caxton material).

Cx 91
Clement Maydeston. *Directorium sacerdotum*^{2}. [1489]
F°. π a^8; a–y^8 z^{10}: 194 leaves. Types 4*, 6.

Duff 292, DeR 78, Blades 80 (87), STC 17722, Cop. 2007, GW 8458.
Cited: Tract Vol. 25 (Cx 91 + 98).

Cx 92
Reynard the Fox[2], tr. William Caxton. [1489]
F°. π[2]; a–h[8] i[6]: 72 leaves. Type 6.
Duff 359, DeR 88, Blades 77 (84), STC 20920, Cop. 398.

Cx 93
Dicts and Sayings of the Philosophers[3], tr. Anthony Woodville, Earl Rivers. [1489]
F°. π[2]; A–G[8] H–I[6]: 70 leaves. Type 6.
Duff 125, DeR 39, Blades 83 (89), STC 6829, Goff D-274, Hain 6285, GW 8323.
Cited: Tract Vols. 19 (Cx 83 + 84 + 93 + 94); 21 (Cx 84 + 93).

Cx 94
The Doctrinal of Sapience, tr. William Caxton. After 7 May 1489.
F°. A–I[8] K–L[10]: 92 leaves. Type 5.
Duff 127, DeR 40, Blades 71 (76), STC 21431, Goff D-302, Hain 14017, GW 8625.
Cited: Tract Vols. 19 (Cx 83 + 84 + 93 + 94); 20 (Cx 83 + 84 + 94); 23 (Cx 83 + ?94); 34 (Cx 83 + 94 + non-Caxton material).

Cx 95
The Mirror of the World[2], tr. William Caxton. [1489]
F°. a–l[8]: 88 leaves. Type 6.
Duff 402, DeR 95, Blades 84 (90), STC 24763, Goff M-884, Hain 11657.
Cited: See Bdr's Waste 10–11.

Cx 96
Pseudo-Bonaventure, i.e., Johannes de Caulibus. *Speculum vitae Christi*[2], English, tr. Nicholas Love. [ca. 1489–90]
F°. a–s[8] t[4]: 148 leaves. Type 5.
Duff 49, DeR 10, Blades 70 (77), STC 3260, Goff B-903, Hain 3564, GW 4764.

Cx 97
The Book of Eneydos, tr. William Caxton. [after 22 June 1490]
F°. A[4] "Aiij"[2]; B–L[8]: 86 leaves. Type 6.
Duff 404, DeR 96, Blades 81 (88), STC 24796, Goff v-199, Cop. 6159.
Cited: Tract Vols. 15 (Cx 58 + 59 + 73 + 97); 26 (Cx 56 + 61 + 64 + 97 + non-Caxton material); 37 (Cx 48 + 59 + 90 + 97 + non-Caxton material).

Cx 98
The Art and Craft of Dying, tr. William Caxton. [after 15 June 1490]

F°. A[8] B[4] "Biij"[2]: 14 leaves. Type 6.
Duff 35, DeR 6, Blades 86 (93), STC 789, Hain 4404, GW 2615.
Cited: Tract Vols. 24 (Cx 64 + 74 + 98); 25 (Cx 91 + 98).

Cx 99
The Governal of Health; and John Lydgate. *Medicina stomachi*. [1490]
4°. A–B[8] [C[2]]: 18 leaves. Type 6.
Duff 165, DeR 47, Blades 76 (83), STC 12138, Goff G-328, Cop. 2765.
Cited: Tract Vol. 28 (Cx 99 + 109 + non-Caxton material).

Cx 100
The Four Sons of Aymon, tr. William Caxton. [1490]
F°. A–Z aa–ll[8] mm[6]: 278 leaves. Type 6.
Duff 152, DeR 45, Blades 79 (86), STC 1007, Hain 2230, GW 3141.

Cx 101
Blanchardin and Eglantine, tr. William Caxton. [1490]
F°. π[6]; A–M[8] . . .: 102+ leaves. Type 6.
Duff 45, DeR 7, Blades 78 (85), STC 3124, Hain 3226, GW 4402.

Cx 102
Statutes: 1, 3, 4 Henry VII. [1491]
F°. a–d[8] e[10]: 42 leaves. Type 6.
Duff 380, DeR 93, Blades 75 (82), STC 9348, Hain 14994.
Cited: Tract Vols. 30 (Cx 102 + non-Caxton material); 31 (Cx 102 + non-Caxton material); 32 (Cx 102 + non-Caxton material).

Cx 103
John Mirk. *Festial*[2]. [1491]
F°. a–p[8] q[2] r[8] s[6]: 136 leaves. Types 6, 8.
Duff 301, DeR 80, Blades 88 (95), STC 17959 (pt. 1), Goff M-621, Hain 7028 (pt. 1).
Cited: Headnote to Appendix B.

Cx 104
Quattuor sermones[3], English. [1491]
F°. A–C[8] D[10]: 34 leaves. Type 6.
Duff 302, DeR 86, Blades 89 (96), STC 17959 (pt. 2), Goff Q-15, Hain 7028 (pt. 2).
Cited: Headnote to Appendix B.

Cx 105
The Fifteen Oes. [1491]
4°. a–b[8] c[6]: 22 leaves. Type 6.
Duff 150, DeR 44, Blades 82 (92), STC 20195, Cop. 4837.
Cited: Tract Vol. 35 (Cx 105 + non-Caxton material); see also Bdr's Waste 10–11.

Cx 106
Sarum Hours. [1491]

4°. Quired in 8s; total of leaves unknown. Type 8.
STC 15872 (note).
Cited: See Bdr's Waste 10–11.

Cx 107

Sarum *Hours.* [1491]
8°. Quired in 8s; total of leaves unknown. Type 8.
STC 15872 (note).
Cited: See Bdr's Waste 10–11.

Cx 108

The Book of Divers Ghostly Matters. [1491]
4°. A–M⁸; ²A–²D⁸; aa–bb⁸ cc⁴: 148 leaves. Type 6.
Duff 55, DeR 12, Blades 85 (91), STC 3305, Goff G-301,
Hain 7771.
Cited: Tract Vol. 29 (Cx 108 + non-Caxton material).

Cx 109

Ars moriendi, English. [1491]
4°. A⁸: 8 leaves. Types 6, 8.
Duff 33, DeR 5, Blades (97), STC 786, Cop. 671, GW 2634.
Cited: Tract Vol. 28 (Cx 99 + 109 + non-Caxton material).

PARIS

Cx 110

Sarum *Missal.* Paris: Guillaume Maynial for William Caxton. 4 December 1487.
F°. π¹⁰; a¹⁰ b–z & 9 A–F⁸ G⁶: 266 leaves. Maynial's type 1
(illus. Claudin II, 2–4).
Duff 322, DeR 102, Blades (103), STC 16164, Cop. 4226.

Cx 111

Sarum *Lectionary.* Paris: Guillaume Maynial for William Caxton. 14 August 1488.
F°. [?π¹⁰] a–y⁸ z⁶; A–X⁸ Y⁶ Z⁴; ²a⁸ ²b⁴: 372 leaves [382, if there was a preliminary calendar of 10 leaves]. Maynial's type 1.
Duff 247, DeR 101, STC 16136, GW 5447.
See Paul Morgan and G. D. Painter, "The Caxton Legenda at St. Mary's, Warwick," *The Library*, 5th ser., 12 (1957): 225–39.

[Caxton: I. Translations]

Le Grand, Jacques. *Book of Good Manners.* Translated from French, finished 8 June 1486. Printed 11 May 1487: Cx 84

Doctrinal of Sapience. Translated from French, finished 7 May 1489. Printed later 1489: Cx 94

Christine de Pisan. *Fayts of Arms.* Translated from French, begun 23 January and finished 7 July 1489. Printed 14 July 1489: Cx 90

Art and Craft of Dying. Translated from French, finished 15 June 1490. Printed later 1490: Cx 98

Book of Eneydos. Translated from French, finished 22 June 1490. Printed later 1490: Cx 97

Blanchardin and Eglantine. Translated from French, ca. 1490? Printed 1490: Cx 101

Life of Robert Earl of Oxford "with divers and many great miracles." Translated from French, ca. 1489–90? Neither the French text nor Caxton's version has been found. Caxton mentions it in his preface to *Four Sons of Aymon,* next below.

Four Sons of Aymon. Translated from French, ca. 1489–90? Printed 1490: Cx 100

Jerome (pseudo-). *Vitas patrum.* Translated from French. Caxton's version, which he "finished . . . at the last day of his life," autumn of 1491, was printed by Wynkyn de Worde in 1495 (Duff 235, STC 14507, Goff H-213).

II. Prologues and epilogues, in chronological order.

Le Fèvre, Raoul. *Recuyell of the Histories of Troy.* [1473–74]. Translated at request of Margaret of York, duchess of Burgundy, sister of Edward IV. (Blake, p. 97): Cx 4

Cessolis, Jacobus de. *Game and Play of Chess.* 31 March 1474. Presented to George, duke of Clarence, brother of Edward IV. (Blake, p. 87): Cx 5, 57

Le Fèvre, Raoul. *History of Jason.* [1477]. Presented to Edward, Prince of Wales, with commendation of his father, Edward IV. (Blake, p. 103): Cx 25

Advertisement for Sarum Ordinal. [1477]. (Blake, p. 55): Cx 24

Dicts and Sayings of the Philosophers. Before 18 November 1477. Printed at request of the translator, Anthony Woodville, Earl Rivers. (Blake, p. 73): Cx 26, 38, 93

[Caxton: II. Prologues and epilogues]

Christine de Pisan. *Moral Proverbs.* 20 February 1478. Printed at request of the translator, Anthony Woodville, Earl Rivers. (Blake, p. 119): Cx 30

Boethius. *Consolation of Philosophy.* [1478]. Printed "at request of a singular friend and gossib of mine" (perhaps William Pratt), and with homage to Chaucer. (Blake, p. 58): Cx 31

Gerard of Vliederhoven. *Cordiale.* 24 March 1479. Printed at request of the translator, Anthony Woodville, Earl Rivers. (Blake, p. 70): Cx 34

Chronicles of England. 10 June 1480. Printed "at request of divers gentlemen." (Blake, p. 68): Cx 39, 53

Description of Britain. 18 August 1480. (Blake, p. 72): Cx 40

Doctrine to Learn French and English. [1480]. (Blake, p. 142): Cx 41

Cicero. *Of Old Age,* etc. 12 August [–ca. Sept.] 1481. Printed under the protection of Edward IV; with pious commemoration of one of the translators, John Tiptoft, earl of Worcester, executed in 1470 during the brief restoration of Henry VI. (Blake, p. 120): Cx 45

Mirror of the World. [ca. October 1481]. Translated at request and cost of Hugh Bryce, alderman of London, for presentation to William, Lord Hastings. (Blake, p. 114): Cx 46, 95

Godfrey of Boloyne. 20 November 1481. Presented to Edward IV, and with commendation of his two sons. (Blake, p. 137): Cx 48

Reynard the Fox. [1482]. (Blake, p. 134): Cx 51, 92

Higden, Ranulph. *Polycronicon.* After 2 July 1482. Translated under the protection of Edward IV. (Blake, p. 128): Cx 52

Chaucer, Geoffrey. *Canterbury Tales.* [2d ed., 1483]. With homage to Chaucer; text corrected at instance of a "gentleman." (Blake, p. 61): Cx 55

Chartier, Alain. *Curial.* [1483]. Translated at request of "a noble and virtuous Earl," probably Anthony Woodville, Earl Rivers. (Blake, p. 72): Cx 58

Chaucer, Geoffrey. *Book of Fame.* [1483]. (Blake, p. 102): Cx 59

Lydgate, John. *Life of Our Lady.* [1483]. (Blake, p. 113): Cx 63

CONCORDANCES

Hain - Copinger - Blades - De Ricci - Duff - STC - Goff

HAIN	CX	HAIN	CX	COPINGER	CX
360	70	7029 (pt. 2)	54, 85	32	24
861	51	7042	6	385	7
1864	80	7048	4	398	92
2230	100	7050	9	671	109
2498	1	7053	25	1178	75
3226	101	7738	2	1457 = 5538	72
3399	31	7771	108	1536	12
3564	96	7835	66	1712	87
3684	48	8331	64	1797	8
3691 = 14049	83	8659	52	2007	91
4113	3	9180	20	2765	99
4404	98	9784	69	3052	11
4521	81	10352	63	3128	77
4754	68	10353	61	3130	77
4755	56	11656	46	3131	33
4901	57	11657	95	3294	88
4902	5	12077	71	3295	89
4918	58	14017	94	3447 = 5501	
4921	17	14048	10	3698	14
4922	55	14049 = 3691		3701	13
4925	59	14994	102	3754	84
4926	60	15607	41	3801	78
4927 (pts. 1–2)	15	15918 = 4988		4226	110
4927 (pts. 3–4)	22			4496	23
4927 (pt. 5)	19			4605	82
4927 (pts. 6–7)	18			4837	105
4927 (pt. 8)	21			4838	74
4927 (pts. 9–11)	27			4925	47
4927 (pt. 12)	29			5270	32
4927 (pts. 13–15)	28			5443	37
4987	30			5444	86
4988 = 15918	90			5501 = 3447	36
5000 (pt. 1)	39			5506	49
5000 (pt. 2)	40			5507	50
HAIN	CX			5538 = 1457	
5002	53			6159	97
5311	45			6472–73	67
5714	34			6583	73
6271	76				
6284	26				
6285	93				
7028 (pt. 1)	103				
7028 (pt. 2)	104				
7029 (pt. 1)	65				

BLADES	CX	BLADES	CX	DeR	CX
1	4	50 (53)	66	1	5
2 (3)	5	51 (54)	69	2	8
3 (2)	6	52 (55)	68	3	4
4	9	53 (56)	67	3b	6
5	7	54 (57)	74	3c	9
6	8	55 (58)	70	3d	7
7 (12)	10	56 (59)	71	4	70
8 (18)	20	57 (60)	55	5	109
9 (7)	25	58 (61)	59	6	98
10 (8)	26	59 (62)	58	7	101
11 (9)	11	60 (63)	60	8	31
12 (10)	17	61 (64)	63	9	75
13 (11)	30	62 (65)	73	10	96
14 (13)	15	63 (66)	80	11	29
15 (14)	22	64 (67)	81	12	108
16 (15)	12	65 (68)	82	13	22
17 (16)	18	66 (69)	67	14	12
18 (17)	14	67 (74)	83	15	56
19	21	68 (70)	84	16	68
20	19	69 (72)	76	17	24
21	13	70 (71, 77)	75, 96	18	57
22	27	71 (76)	94	19	81
23	29	72 (73, 80)	77	20	58
24	28	73 (79)	86	21	59
25	31	74 (81)	90	22	17
26	34	75 (82)	102	23	55
27	32	76 (83)	99	24	28
28	38	77 (84)	92	25	27
29	36	78 (85)	101	26	60
30	56	79 (86)	100	27	30
31	46	80 (87)	91	28	90
32	51	81 (88)	97	29	39
33	45	82 (92)	105	30	53
34	57	83 (89)	93	31	45
35	24	84 (90)	95	32	87
36	23	85 (91)	108	33	34
37	33	86 (93)	98	34	74
38	47	88 (95)	103	35	40
39	39	89 (96)	104	36–37	26
40	40	(44)	50	38	38
40* (43)	49	(52)	72	39	93
41	61	(78)	87	40	94
42	48	(97)	109	41	78
43 (45)	53	(103)	110	42	86
44 (46)	52			43	37
45 (47)	64			44	105
46 (48)	41			45	100
47 (49)	65			46	48
48 (50)	54, 85			47	99
49 (51)	37			48	66

DeR	CX		DUFF	CX		DUFF	CX
49	52		4	70		175	33
50	11		25	7		178–79	77
51	33		33	109		204	36
52–53	77		35	98		207	43
56	36		39	1		209	50
57	43		45	101		210	49
58	50		47	31		211	88
59	49		48	75		212	89
60	88		49	96		222	20
61	89		53	29		241	69
62	20		55	108		242	4
63	69		58	71		243	6
64	25		76	22		244	9
65	84		77	12		245	25
66	19		78	56		247	111
67	13		79	68		248	84
68	61		80	24		256	19
69	18		81	5		257	13
70	14		82	57		260	61
71	63		83	81		261	18
72	62		84	58		262	14
73	64		86	59		266	63
74	15		87	17		266a	62
75	21		88	55		267	64
76	80		92	28		269	15
77	76		93	27		270	21
78	91		94	60		283	80
79	65		95	30		290	76
80	103		96	90		292	91
81	71		97	39		298	65
82	23		98	53		299	54, 85
83	82		103	45		301	103
84	47		105	87		302	104
85	54, 85		108	8		322	110
86	104		109	34		336	23
87	51		112	74		337	82
88	92		113	40		354	47
89	83		123	26		358	51
90	10		124	38		359	92
91	32		125	93		366	83
92	72		127	94		367	10
93	102		129	78		368	32
94	46		146	86		371	72
95	95		148	37		380	102
96	97		150	105		401	46
97	41		152	100		402	95
98–99	67		164	48		404	97
100	73		165	99		405	41
101	111		166	66		408–9	67
102	110		172	52		414	73
			174	11			

STC	CX	STC	CX	STC	CX
175	70	14077 c.114		24190.3	35
786	109	(formerly 14100)	88	24762	46
789	98	14077 c.113		24763	95
801	80	(formerly 22587)	49	24796	97
1007	100	14077 c.106	16	24865	41
3124	101	14077 c.107		24873–74	67
3199	31	(formerly 22582)	36	25853	73
3259	75	14551	20		
3260	96	14554	74		
3303	29	15296	69		
3305	108	15375	4		
3326	71	15383	25		
4850	22	15394	84		
4851	12	15848	37		
4852	56	15854	86		
4853	68	15867	11		
4890	24	15868	33		
4920	5	15871–72	77		
4921	57	15872 (note)	106		
5013	81	15872 (note)	107		
5057	58	16136	111		
5082	17	16164	110		
5083	55	16228	23		
5087	59	16253	47		
5090	28	17008	19		
5091	27	17009	13		
5094	60	17015	61		
5293	45	17018	18		
5758	34	17019	14		
6473–74	64	17023	63		
6826–27	26	17024	62		
6828	38	17030	15		
6829	93	17032	21		
7013	78	17534	87		
7269	90	17720	76		
7273	30	17722	91		
9348	102	17957 (pt. 1)	65		
9991	39	17957 (note)	54		
9992	53	17957 (note)	85		
12138	99	17959 (pt. 1)	103		
12142	66	17959 (pt. 2)	104		
13175	48	19206	82		
13438	52	20195	105		
13440a	40	20919	51		
14077 c.110		20920	92		
(formerly 22584)	43	21429	83		
14077 c.115		21431	94		
(formerly 14101)	89	21548	10		
14077 c.112		22588	72		
(formerly 22586)	50	24188.5 = 24189	32		

GOFF	CX
B–131	1
B–813	31
B–903	96
B–1318	3
C–313	68
C–314	12
C–413	5
C–414	57
C–429	58
C–431	17
C–432	55
C–472	90
C–473	30
C–477 (pt. 1)	39
C–477 (pt. 2)	40
C–478	53
C–627	45
C–907	34
C–908	8
D–272	26
D–273	38
D–274	93
D–302	94
G–281	2
G–301	108
G–316	48
G–328	99
G–329	66
G–640	64
H–267	52
H–420	11
I–73	20
I–123	88
J–148–49	67
L–72	69
L–91	83
L–112	25
L–113	6
L–117	4
L–406	13
L–407	14
L–409	63
L–410	62
L–411	15
M–103	80
M–620	65
M–621	103
M–883	46
M–884	95
O–93	71

GOFF	CX
Q–14	85
Q–15	104
R–137	51
S–565	50
V–199	97
V–315	41
W–62	73

The Printer & the Pardoner has been composed
in Monotype Bembo and printed and bound by
Meriden-Stinehour Press in Lunenburg, Vermont
The design is by Stephen Harvard